Guide

MW01133074

WORLD WAR ONE SOLDIERS

Laurent MIROUZE

This guide only deals with soldiers from the main belligerent countries of WW1. Due to lack of space, soldiers from the Commonwealth, for instance, or serving outside Europe have been left out.

HISTOIRE & COLLECTIONS

BELGIAN INFANTRYMAN, AUGUST 1914

The small Belgian army resisted the first German offensive gallantly, but heroic resistance could not outweigh the massive advantage in number and resources enjoyed by the invaders.

The silhouette of the Belgian infantryman of 1914 was one of the most archaic in Western Europe: the felt shako, heavy greatcoat, large cartridge pouch and unwieldy knapsack contributed to his generally old-fashioned appearance. As in neighbouring France, the high command had been slow to modernise the army, and it was unfortunate that the first of the planned reforms of uniform and equipment was interrupted by the outbreak of hostilities. It immediately became evident that the Belgian soldier's outfit was badly suited to modern warfare, and the first changes were forced through after a matter of weeks. These involved a general simplification, dictated as much by economy as by battlefield conditions.

1 - Black felt M1893 shako, its brass plate bearing the regimental number. In field dress it was covered with this black oilcloth sleeve with a white-painted number, here for the 9th Line Infantry. The broad chin strap and red wool tuft dated from the 19th century.

2 - Dark blue M1906 greatcoat of heavy wool, in a shade known as 'gros bleu'. It had a turned-down collar, and fastened by two rows of five brass buttons bearing the regimental number. On each side a brass hook helped support the weight of the belt; and there were two large side pockets with single-button flaps. The rear vent could be closed by two buttons; a two-button half-belt adjusted the fit at the waist, and the skirts could be buttoned back to free the legs on the march. Obscured by the coat in these photos is a tunic of similar colour, fastened by a single row of six buttons. Its buttons were the only indication of the unit.

3 - Black satin stock edged with leather, protecting the neck from chafing against the greatcoat.

4 - Heavy grey-blue wool M1906/11 trousers, cut straight, with vertical slash side pockets; a half-belt allowed for adjustment at the waist.

5 - Black leather M1896 belt. The rectangular brass plate, obscured here, was worn slightly to the left of centre because of the position of the pouch.

6 - Black leather M1896 cartridge pouch, its flap fastened at the rear by two brass studs. Two rear hooks engaged with the front braces of the knapsack, as illustrated.

7 - Black leather bayonet frog with hilt tab. The bayonet scabbard was often strapped upon the entrenching tool in the German fashion.

8 - M1896 knapsack of cow hide, bound with black leather and lined with grey cloth, and with a compartmented cane framework. It contained a change of clothes and reserve rations. Four straps allowed for outer stowage of the bedroll and spare boots.

9 - Black-painted aluminium mess tin, inspired by the German pattern; a spoon the doubled as a handle. Contents: 2.5 liters. The tin was affixed to the knapsack by means of a black leather strap.

10 - Brown cloth M1896 bread bag, with leather belt loops. It featured three internal pockets, and a strap and ring on the flap for the water bottle. The bag could also be slung round the body thanks to a cloth loops.

11 - Water bottle in aluminium covered with brown wool, hooked onto the bread bag. Of one litre capacity, the water bottle too resembled the contemporary German issue.

12 - Entrenching tool, Linnemann pattern, suspended from the belt by means of a black leather carrier with two straps.

13 - Black leather M1891 anklets, laced up the front by means of metal hooks.

14 - M1910 issue shoes in blackened leather.

15 - Mauser M1889 rifle of 7.65 mm calibre.

GERMAN INFANTRYMAN, AUGUST 1914

This senior corporal of Infantry Regiment 'Herwarth von Bittenfeld' (1st Westphalian) No 13 represents the classic German soldier. Although he has recently been outfitted with a modern uniform of neutral 'Feldgrau' colour, he retains elements handed down through a long military tradition, and evocative of the war of 1870-71 against France. The spiked helmet and the knee-length marching boots had been in use for generations in the Prussian, and later the German army, and retained an old-fashioned look in 1914. Nevertheless, the iron discipline of the Kaiser's army, and its excellent equipment - particularly the formidable MG08 machine gun, which decimated the French infantry - quickly dispelled any illusions about Germany's readiness for war.

1 - M1895 Pickelhaube helmet, the latest in a series of similar helmets stretching back to 1842. It was made of leather, with brass spike and fittings, and offered little protection. On campaign, the M1892 helmet cover, with a red cut-out regimental number, concealed the bright metal plate – which varied according to the regiment – and the side cockades (one in the Imperial colours and the other in the colours of the Land or State).

2 - M1907/10 tunic in 'field grey' cloth, fastening with a single row of eight buttons whose colour and design varied according to the regiment. Most infantry regiments had the turned-down collar, the front edge, and the simulated three-button pocket flaps in the tails piped in red. The cuff flaps varied in design according to unit, but often, as here, were of 'Brandenburg' shape, and adorned with three buttons. This NCO's status is shown by gold braid round the collar and cuffs. The detachable field grey shoulder straps were piped in colours identifying the Army Corps, and bore a red number or monogram for the regiment.

3 - M1895 belt in tan leather, flesh side out. The plate varied according to the Land, here it is Prussian, in brass with a white metal central device bearing the Prussian crown and 'Gott Mit Uns' motto.

4 - M1909 cartridge pouches in pebbled brown leather. Each of the six pockets, in two sets of three, holds four five-round clips of 7.92 mm cartridges, for a total of 120 rounds. The weight is distributed by means of a ring on the back, attached to a hook at the end of the knapsack braces.

5 - M1895 knapsack in cow hide, the flap faced with unshaven hide. All leather parts are brown, and the pack has a wooden frame. The knapsack accommodated changes of clothes, blankets, off-duty footwear, reserve rations, etc. The outer stowage comprised the grey M1907 greatcoat and the M1892 tan-coloured tent section. The M1910 mess tin in black-painted aluminium was held to the flap by two brown straps.

6 - M1887 'bread bag', in light brown canvas; suspended from the belt by two buttoned loops and a central tab and flat hook. Two rings on the back allowed the attachment of a strap so that it could also be slung round the body. The bag held rations, eating utensils as well as small personal effects.

7 - The M1907 water bottle of cloth-covered aluminium, hooked to the bread bag.

8 - M1887 entrenching tool and leather carrier, suspended from the belt on the left side. The strap securing the handle also held the bayonet scabbard. The latter is the M1898 in steel-reinforced leather. The bayonet knot is the NCO's pattern in silver wire.

9 - M1907/10 trousers in field grey cloth, with red piping down the outer seams. These had two diagonal side slash pockets, a small fob pocket and a half-belt for waist adjustment.

10- M1866 tan leather marching boots, flesh side out.

11 - M1898 Mauser rifle, 7.92 mm calibre.

12 - M1898 bayonet. Theoretically, NCOs were issued with a special pattern with a sawtoothed back edge.

FRENCH INFANTRYMAN, AUGUST 1914

The unsuitability of the French infantryman's uniform for modern warfare came as no surprise in 1914. Since the Boer War of 1899-1902 had demonstrated the importance of a drab field uniform, French reformers had been pressing for a radical modification of issue clothing, as much of the cut as the colours. Between 1903 and 1914 many trials were carried out with uniforms of drab, blue-grey, blue-beige and yellow weed colour, but none were adopted. Ironically, a decision was finally reached on 27 July 1914, just six days before the outbreak of war. The French infantryman suffered through the first months in a uniform which had hardly changed since the Franco-Prussian War. Ordered against German machine guns in mad bayonet charges, the 'red trousers' fell like corn before the scythe, until the miraculous recovery on the Marne river.

1 - M1884 képi, with dark blue band and red top, rounded visor and chin strap of black leather, and regimental number applied to the band in red cut-out digits. The blue cloth field cover, the sole concession to modern warfare, dated from 1913.

2 - Blue cotton stock, knotted like a cravat.

3 - M1877 greatcoat in heavy 'iron blue-grey' cloth. Hardly changed since the Second Empire, it was double-breasted, with two rows of six half-ball buttons of yellow metal bearing a grenade device. There was a half-belt for adjustment, and two rear pockets with access via the long central vent. The skirts were buttoned back to free the legs, and buttoned slits allowed the cuffs to be turned up. The low, uncomfortable standing collar bore red patches, with the regimental number in cut-out blue-grey figures. This man has the two large red cuff stripes of a corporal. The shoulders sport detachable rolled straps, M1913, designed to hold the various slings and braces.

4 - Lebel rifle equipment in black leather, flesh side out, which incorporated the old belt with its brass plate, and comprised:
- Three M1888 or M1905 cartridge pouches (differing only in the design of their belt loops), two front and one in the back.
- Y-shaped M1892 braces, fixed to the back of each pouch by a brass hook.
- M1888 frog for the Lebel's spike bayonet. This was suspended from the belt on the left side, but this and the blackened bronze scabbard are obscured here by the haversack and the coat turn-back.

5 - M1893 knapsack with black leather straps and tabs, and a rigid wooden frame. It had hardly changed since the days of Louis-Napoleon. In August 1914 the exterior stowage no longer included blankets or tent section, but was limited to a pair of off-duty shoes in a bag, and the M1882 round mess tin – slightly tilted so not to hit the soldier's head when firing in the prone position; an entrenching tool on the left side – here the Seurre pattern; and one of the rifle section's cooking utensils. Rather than the large dixie or the flat pan, this man carries the loaf of bread which represented a section's daily ration.

6 - M1892 sidebag in tan canvas, containing daily rations, eating utensils, and - in theory - the cup, which in practice was usually strung to the water bottle.

7 - One-litre M1877 water bottle with two spouts, made of tinned iron and covered with salvaged coat material. It was normally slung on the right side, and the bag on the left.

8 - Madder red wool trousers, M1867 modified in 1893 and 1897; the changes had been minimal. The straight-cut trousers had a pocket cut in each side seam, one right fob pocket, and a rear half-belt for adjustment.

9 - M1913 gaiters in black leather, lacing up the front by means of hooks and eyes; these were adopted after numerous experiments, beginning in 1897.

10 - Black leather ankle boots. Various patterns were in use in 1914, principally the high topped model with six pairs of eyelets, adopted in 1893. The more recent 1912 pattern had a lower shaft and seven pairs of eyelets.

11 - M1886/93 Lebel rifle of 8 mm calibre; this weapon relied upon the out-dated Kropatschek action, with eight rounds in a tubular magazine under the barrel. The M1886 spike bayonet featured a German silver hilt and a curved quillon.

BRITISH INFANTRYMAN, AUGUST 1914

On the eve of the Great War, the British Army was extremely well equipped and armed. The lessons of the most recent colonial campaigns had been learned, particularly those taught at such murderous cost by the Boers in 1899-1902. The most obvious reform was the adoption of a simple, practical and inconspicuous uniform of drab brown cloth. The individual equipment was innovative in both its material and its design. The former was the strong cotton webbing first seen in the 1880s, when Capt. Anson Mills of the US Army used it for improved cartridge belts. The various equipment components were now arranged in an integrated system giving reasonable distribution of weight. The soldier's weapon was also well suited for modern warfare: the Short Magazine Lee Enfield rifle No 1 Mark III of .303 in. calibre, with a ten-round removable box magazine allowing sustained rapid fire. Despite its small numbers, the British Expeditionary Force put up a strong resistance to the German divisions which poured into Belgium and northern France in the summer of 1914.

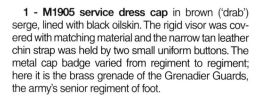

1 - M1905 service dress cap in brown ('drab') serge, lined with black oilskin. The rigid visor was covered with matching material and the narrow tan leather chin strap was held by two small uniform buttons. The metal cap badge varied from regiment to regiment; here it is the brass grenade of the Grenadier Guards, the army's senior regiment of foot.

2 - M1902 service dress tunic in brown serge, of simple and practical cut, which hardly changed until 1937. The turned-down collar was closed by one or two hooks and eyes. There were four front pockets with straight buttoned flaps, the chest pockets being pleated. The shoulders were reinforced against the weight and chafing of the equipment with rectangular patches. There were two short rear vents. The only unit insignia at this date were the brass regimental titles, pinned to the shoulder straps. As an exception, this Grenadier guardsman sports embroidered cloth titles in white on red, sewn to the top of the sleeves.

3 - M1902 service dress trousers in brown serge. These straight-cut trousers had two vertical slash side pockets; they were worn with braces, and had 12 buttons arranged round the waist for this purpose.

4 - M1908 cotton webbing equipment, carrying all the soldier's field necessities by means of an interconnected system adjusted by buckled straps. It could be donned or doffed in one piece by unfastening the belt. The separate items could be arranged in a number of different ways; the set illustrated is the 'marching order' for a rifleman.

On the left hip is the **haversack**, containing rations, eating utensils and personal effects. Under this are the bayonet, with the entrenching tool helve attached to it.

On the right hip are the **entrenching tool** head in its carrier, beneath the **water bottle**. Of two-pint capacity, it is made of enamelled steel covered with brown wool. On the chest, left and right, are two sets each of five **cartridge carriers**; each accommodated three five-round charger clips, for a total load of 150.

Attached to the shoulder braces and to diagonal straps projecting backwards from the cartridge carrier sets is the **pack** or 'valise', containing the greatcoat, changes of clothing, etc. The crossed diagonal straps allowed exterior stowage. The whole set was based upon a broad waist belt, and broad shoulder braces crossing on the back.

5 - M1902 cloth puttees, secured by tapes.

6 - 'Ammunition boots,' blackened for service dress but often unblackened and dubbined for field use.

7 - SMLE No 1 Mark III rifle, calibre .303 in. This bolt-action rifle, in the hands of the long-service regulars of the BEF, was capable of very rapid, accurate fire, and was a byword for sturdiness and reliability.

8 - M1908 webbing rifle sling.

RUSSIAN INFANTRYMAN, AUGUST 1914

The Russo-Japanese War of 1904-05 had ended in disaster for the Russian army, and the necessity of reforming its uniforms and equipment was clear. Czar Nicholas II took a personal interest in the issue and by the outbreak of the Great War, the long-suffering Russian soldier had been provided with a much more practical outfit and lightened field gear. Some elements of this uniform and equipment were still prevalent, in developed form, until the 1980s. The regulations accompanying the new uniform (which was brown from 1908) called for a military version of the traditional Russian shirt-tunic ('Gymnastierka'), breeches, and a visored cap. A heavier version of the same dress was issued for the winter. The soft leather knee-boots and 'horseshoe' roll completed the typical image of the Russian soldier.

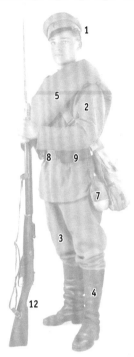

1 - M1907/10 cap in cotton or linen, with a leather peak. Leather chin straps, although not regulation, were often added. The pressed tin cockade is painted in the orange and black Imperial colours.

2 - M1912 'Gymnastierka', a long, baggy shirt-tunic traditionally worn by the Russian peasantry, here in khaki drill for the warm seasons. The stand collar fastened with two small offset buttons. This 'pullover' garment had a front vent from collar to mid-chest only, fastened by two or three small buttons. There were many variations of detail, given the dispersed manufacture of uniforms: typical differences included chest pockets, gathered cuffs, button placing on the collar or chest, etc. The characteristic shoulder boards were rigid and removable, bearing the unit's number or monogram.

3 - M1907 breeches, cut full in the thigh and tight at the knee, and made in khaki-green drill or wool depending on the season. There were two vertical side pockets.

4 - The breeches tucked into black soft leather **knee-boots**, which were worn by all personnel apart from certain troops such as bicycle units.

5 - Tent section and greatcoat, rolled together and carried in horseshoe fashion. The M1911 greatcoat was a straight, single-breasted garment fastened by five brass buttons embossed with the Imperial eagle; it had straight cuffs, and a half-belt with two adjustment buttons.

6 - The ends of the horseshoe roll were strapped tightly together and stuffed into the round **M1909 mess tin**, made of copper alloy.

7 - M1909 aluminium **water bottle** covered with brown wool. The soldier's cup fitted on the bottom of the bottle; the latter being slung round the body thanks to a leather strap.

8 - Leather belt, with a brass plate charged with the two-headed Imperial eagle, of the type adopted in 1904.

9 - M1893 brown leather **cartridge pouches**; each of the pair accommodated six five-round clips, giving a total load of 60 rounds of rifle ammunition.

10 - Linnemann pattern **entrenching tool**, here in a leather carrier. The tool soldiered on to the Second World War, but the carrier was made in various materials, often in canvas.

11 - M1910 sidebag, made of greyish beige waterproofed cloth, the straps of leather. It was normally slung round the body, but the sling could be arranged in such a way that it could be worn on the back like a knapsack. The usual contents were rations, spare clothing, such as the footcloths wrapped round the feet inside the boots, small personal effects, and 40 additional rifle rounds.

12 - M1891 Mosin Nagant rifle, calibre 7.62 mm, of the model known as 'three-line'. The long socket bayonet, M1891, was permanently fixed; the rifle sling was of leather.

SCOTTISH INFANTRYMAN, SEPTEMBER 1914

The Scottish Highlander was perhaps the most visually striking of all the Allied soldiers in 1914. The same loyalty to tradition which made him such a formidable fighting man had preserved elements of his national costume — most noticeably the Glengarry bonnet with its diced band, and the kilt. Only the Highland units — traditionally, but by then not exclusively recruited in the hills of northern and western Scotland - retained the kilt. In 1914 there were five Highland regiments, which were distinguished one from the other by differences in the Glengarry, kilt and hose tops patterns; the rest of the uniform was almost identical to that of British regiments. The uniform illustrated is that of the Seaforth Highlanders, whose 2nd Battalion was one of eight Highland units despatched to France in August 1914 with the BEF.

1 - The Glengarry had been specified for all infantry regiments in the 1860s as undress headgear. In most Scottish regiments it was retained instead of the new service dress cap, until replaced by the drab wool Tam o' Shanter in 1915. The Seaforths wore the usual dark blue ribboned bonnet, with a red 'Toorie' (tuft), a red, white and blue diced band, and the regimental badge pinned upon a silk ribbon.

2 - M1902 service dress tunic, of the 'doublet' cut issued to Scottish regiments, with rounded front skirts. The standard tunic was often issued as the war progressed, and tailored at unit level. The only insignia worn in 1914 were the brass shoulder titles.

3 - M1908 webbing equipment, as described on page 10. The assembly of this 'marching order' was as follows:

– The bayonet frog was slid onto the belt on the left hip; the entrenching tool helve holder was buckled to it. The left and right pouch sets were fitted to the belt.

– Two shoulder braces were buckled to the rear of the pouches, leaving a length protruding below the belt. The braces passed over the shoulders, crossed in the back, and passed through buckles on the back of the belt. This left four brace ends hanging, at left front and back, and right front and back.

– The right side ends received the entrenching tool head carrier, the end tabs engaging on the water bottle carrier.

– The haversack was buckled onto the ends hanging on the left side, over the bayonet and tool helve.

– The 'valise' was attached by two buckles to the upper portion of the shoulder braces. Two narrow straps extending from the rear of the ammunition pouch sets engaged with the buckles of the two external pack straps, which were anchored by loops under the valise at each side. These external straps crossed over the valise and buckled on its inner top. The whole weight of the ammunition, belt kit and pack was thus distributed as evenly as possible.

4 - The kilt, a piece of pleated woollen cloth about seven yards long, wound round the waist so as to leave the unpleated part at the front, and secured with two buckled straps at the side. Each regiment had its own distinctive tartan, in the case of the Seaforths the Mackenzie sett. In field dress, the kilt was protected by a plain drill cover.

5 - The kilt cover, a light brown apron which completely obscured the colourful tartan of the kilt, fastened by buckles on the right. In front a large pocket with a pointed flap replaced the full and walking-out dress Sporran.

6 - In 1914 men of kilted regiments could also be distinguished by the particular pattern of their checkered woollen '**hose tops**'. These were rapidly replaced however by less conspicuous khaki stockings.

7 - The hose-tops or stockings were held up by garters, with visible **flashes** of different shapes and colours depending on the unit.

8 - Canvas gaiters, of the old 'spatterdash' pattern, covered the stockings and boots at the beginning of the war. They were soon replaced by puttees. The gaiters had eight side buttons and a leather strap on the instep.

9 - Hobnailed ammunition boots.

10 - No 1 Mark III rifle, calibre .303 in.

FRENCH INFANTRYMAN, SPRING 1915

In the aftermath of the battle of the Marne, France more than any other nation faced the urgent necessity of re-equipping her army for a war which was evidently going to last much longer than had been expected. A new uniform, cut from symbolically termed 'tricolour cloth' and woven of a mixture of red, white and blue yarns, had been chosen a few days before the outbreak of war, but never issued. Ironically, it turned out that all the dyes - even the famous 'garance' (madder red) seen on trousers and képis - were obtained from Germany; and France was reduced to seizing the stocks of the French subsidiary of a German company. Indigo blue was readily available, but not alizarine red for 'garance.' The new weave was therefore reduced to two colours, blue and white; and thus, by the chances of war, was born the light blue shade which passed into history as 'horizon blue.'

1 - M1914 képi, a simplified version of the traditional pattern. The cloth used in this example is 'English blue-grey', an imported fabric used in 1914-15 to supplement hard-pressed French resources.

2 - Anti-gas goggles; many varying models were used from May 1915 onwards.

3 - Blue cotton stock; also just visible is the collar of the pre-war dark blue tunic, a nine-button stable jacket with red collar patches bearing dark blue regimental numbers.

4 - M1914 simplified greatcoat in 'horizon blue.' To cut both cost and delivery time the leading fashion designer Paul Poiret produced in September 1914 this single-breasted pattern with six front buttons. The large fall collar bears the yellow patches with dark blue regimental numbers and pipings introduced for the infantry by regulations of 9 December 1914. Some coats had two breast pockets with buttoned flaps, some only one on the right side, as here. Buttons were initially of plain four-hole design; the old pattern charged with a grenade device were later revived, but in white metal painted grey-blue. The dark blue star on the left arm is a non-regulation badge worn by infantry scouts.

5 - Anti-gas pad, here the very first 'Compresse C1', issued in May 1915. The bag, tied by a tape to the coat button, was made of rubberised cloth; it contained a pad of cotton impregnated with hyposulphite and carbonate of soda, which the soldier was supposed to clap over his nose and mouth like a modern smog mask in case of gas alert.

6 - Steel skull protector. Although in some ways slow to modernise, the French army was the first to adopt a modicum of head protection. From March 1915 a 'brain pan' recalling the 17th century 'cervelière' was issued for wear under the képi. This unpopular device was only a stop-gap until the issue of a true helmet, which had been decided upon in February 1915.

7 - Lebel rifle equipment in black leather. This was essentially unchanged since August 1914, apart from the new pattern M1903/14 belt with a two-pronged brass buckle.

8 - Knapsack. Throughout the war the French infantryman would retain the basic pack of 1914, by now completely out of date. From the end of 1914 onward his burden was increased by the addition of rolled blankets and a tent section, complete with pegs and cords. The knapsack illustrated here is a simplified model of wartime manufacture, in grey-blue canvas. An item from the section's field equipment (here, a canvas bucket) and an individual tool (here, the M1879 spade) are attached in regulation manner.

9 - M1892 sidebag, here a wartime example in greenish grey canvas. There were several variations in materials and colours.

10 - M1877 one-litre water bottle, covered in reclaimed grey-blue coat cloth.

11 - M1914 trousers/breeches, loose in the thigh and tight from the knee down, to be worn with puttees. Examples manufactured in late 1914 and early 1915 were often made of coarse corduroy in various drab shades, as horizon blue cloth was then earmarked for képis and greatcoats. Theoretically these trousers should have been worn under the blue overalls issued since 1914 to conceal the old red trousers.

12 - Puttees in neutral drab cloth. Long the mark of the Chasseurs Alpins, these became general issue for foot soldiers at the end of 1914.

13 - M1912 shoes.

14 - M1886/93 Lebel rifle, 8 mm calibre, and its needle bayonet.

GERMAN INFANTRYMAN, APRIL 1915

When the offensives of summer 1914 ground to a halt, and the front lines stabilised for what threatened to be a long war, the German army was forced to reconsider the elaborate uniform which had been devised in peacetime. The huge numbers of men called to arms and their lavish consumption of all kinds of stores took the German quartermaster by surprise, and stockpiles dwindled at alarming rates. The Allied maritime blockade of the Central Powers also created shortages of raw materials from 1915 on, and German industry was compelled to resort to the production of synthetic and substitute materials - the famous 'ersatz' products which gave the world a new term. At the level of the fighting soldier, the most immediate result was the steady replacement of leather by vulcanised fibre, of brass by painted iron, and of uniforms of pre-war quality by simplified designs made of inferior material. The appearance of the German infantryman had thus begun to change by the end of the first year of the war.

1 - M1915 helmet, the last of the spiked *Pickelhaube*, soon to be replaced by an actual steel helmet. In most cases its shell was made of boiled leather, but there were also examples made of felt, compressed cardboard or thin metal (which offered no serious protection). The helmet fittings were in all cases of white metal alloy painted grey. The spike, judged to be too visible, was now removed in field dress. The cloth helmet cover therefore lost its tip and, also for reasons of concealment, its red regimental numbers.

2 - M1914 tunic, a simplified variant of the M1907/10 pattern. The cut was more close-fitting; the shade of the field grey cloth became darker and greener; and the fancy cuff patches and false skirt pocket flaps were omitted. The cuffs themselves became deeper; NCO braid was now displayed only on the collar. The shoulder straps of field grey cloth were piped in white for all infantry formations, with unit numbers or monograms embroidered in red. The straps were let in at the shoulder seam. The black and white ribbon in the second tunic buttonhole is that of the Iron Cross 2nd Class.

3 - M1895 belt, now blackened, and with an iron plate painted field grey; older bi-metal plates were similarly painted over.

4 - M1909 cartridge pouches; the new regulations called for them to be blackened, but the pebbled finish of the leather made this difficult.

5 - The soldier illustrated wears **light field equipment**, without the cumbersome M1895 knapsack. The considerable weight of the cartridge pouches led to the use of the breadbag strap to support them in the absence of the knapsack's braces.

6 - M1915 gasmask. The 'Gummimaske' comprised of a rubberised fabric facepiece and a detachable canister, which were carried (with a spare canister) in a strong cloth bag looped to the belt.

7 - M1915 stick grenade.

8 - M1887 breadbag, in this case a wartime example in poor quality canvas.

9 - M1907 water bottle, also an ersatz in enamelled metal, here covered with brown corduroy, probably of civilian origin. The attachment strap has been reduced to its simplest form.

10 - M1887 spade in its leather carrier, secured to the scabbard of the M1898/1905 bayonet by a strap.

11 - M1914 trousers; these were identical in cut and pocket details to the M1907/10 pattern, but made of 'stone grey' (*Steingrau*) cloth. This was chosen when it was discovered that the Feldgrau trousers rapidly faded in use; this darker shade lasted longer. The red piping down the outer seams was retained.

12 - M1866 marching boots in tan leather; these were blackened from 1915 on.

13 - M1898 Mauser rifle, 7.92 mm calibre.

14 - M1898/1905 bayonet. Originally introduced for the foot artillery, with a leather scabbard, it was issued from 1915 to the infantry with a sturdier metal scabbard, replacing the longer and more fragile M1898 infantry bayonet.

8
9
14
10

BERSAGLIER, ITALIAN FRONT, 1915

Like most European nations, the Italians initiated a radical reform of field uniforms at the beginning of the 20th century. At that date, the kingdom was allied to the Austro-Hungarian Empire and Germany, and the latter's influence – after her prestigious victory of 1870-71 – was considerable. In 1909 Italy adopted, like Austria-Hungary, a uniform colour similar to the German Feldgrau of 1907; in Italy's case this was termed simply 'grigio-verde' (grey-green). The same shade was chosen for leather equipment from 1907 onwards. The light infantry or 'Bersaglieri', established by Captain Alessandro La Marmora in 1836, were an elite corps. These units were repeatedly committed during Italy's 19th century campaigns, and acquired a reputation for dash, courage, and practical experience. During the Great War they were credited with turning the tide in Italy's favour in many battles. Their traditional undress headgear, inherited from Crimean campaigns alongside the Turks, was a crimson fez with a blue tassel.

1 - M1871 Bersaglier hat, of pressed felt and simulated leather, with black and green cockerel feathers on the right side. The cockade in red, white and green bore a stamped brass badge in the shape of a flaming grenade bearing the regimental number, and crossed rifles. In field dress, the hat was fitted with a grey cloth cover bearing the badge embroidered in black on grey-green. The hat was, of course, unsuitable for modern warfare, and was later replaced by the M1916 steel helmet, also adorned with the Bersaglieri plumes.

2 - M1909 tunic in grey-green wool, with a standing collar and fly front. There were no visible external pockets. The cuffs were pointed, and there were two short rear vents closed with a button. Although obscured here, the collar patches were crimson, bearing the star of Savoy worn by all Italian soldiers.

3 - M1909 trousers; these were laced at the ankles, and had two slanted side pockets.

4 - M1909 puttees, which replaced the black gaiters worn at the outbreak of war.

5 - M1912 ankle boots in brown leather; these were provided with cleats for mountain use.

6 - M1912 cape. This short wool garment was issued to all infantry at the outbreak of the war. It had a falling collar fastened with a hook and bearing the ubiquitous star of Savoy; and a single hidden button closure down the front.

7 - M1907 equipment, made of grey-green finished leather. The belt had a plain one-prong buckle. Unusually, the brace to support the belt kit was not the 'Y' or 'X' arrangement favoured in other armies, but a single loop passing round the neck and down the front again. There was a matching bayonet frog; and a pair of double cartridge pouches for the Carcano 6.5 mm ammunition.

8 - M1907 haversack. This was made of canvas with leather fittings and could be arranged either as a knapsack or as a sidebag, as shown here. It accommodated all the soldier's immediate necessities.

9 - M1891 bayonet.

10 - M1891 Carcano carbine, in the 6.5 mm standard calibre. The carbine was originally designed as a cavalry weapon, but was later issued to all light troops. It had a permanently fixed folding bayonet.

BRITISH INFANTRYMAN, OCTOBER 1915

After the retreat from Mons, the harsh winter of 1914-15 found the combatants on both sides holding stabilised front lines; there now began the long agony of trench warfare, which would last until well into 1918. Like the other armies, the British discovered that their issue clothing and equipment needed adaptation to the new realities of static warfare, under increasingly heavy artillery fire, in all weathers. A new army of volunteers was raised in Britain, to replace the very serious losses suffered by the first BEF (up to 90% in most battalions). Due to the unexpected demand for uniforms and equipment, many of these 'Kitchener's army' volunteers had to train in civilian clothing; as stocks intended for training had already been rushed to the front. The Regulars improvised as best they could, and gratefully received goatskin jerkins which made them look like soldiers in the Crimea. The stiff service dress cap now gave way to a soft model with let-down ear and neck flaps, giving better protection. The smart silhouette of 1914 was already changing under pressure of trench conditions.

1 - M 1915 trench cap, popularly known as the 'Gor Blimey', possibly in reference to the reaction of Regular NCOs to its unsoldierly appearance. Essentially similar to the rigid version, it had a soft visor and unstiffened top, and deep neck and ear flaps which buttoned round the face in bad weather, and were turned up and buttoned over the top when not in use. There was no chin strap. Regimental badges were, as before, pinned on the band; this is that of the King's Royal Rifle Corps, on the regimental scarlet cloth backing.

2 - M1902 service dress tunic. In Rifle regiments all badges and buttons were black; note the 'KRR' titles on the shoulder straps. The rifle marksman's badge on the left cuff is in brass, however.

3 - 'PH' type anti-gas hood in its small two-button pocket. Rushed into service after heavy casualties at Ypres on 22-23 April 1915, the phenate-hexamine (PH) flannel hood was impregnated with these chemicals, which supposedly neutralised mustard gas. It was fitted with glass eyepieces, and a rubber exhaust valve.

4 - M1914 equipment in a combination of leather and webbing. Originally intended for training only, it was issued in large numbers to the new volunteer battalions due to a shortage of webbing gear. It comprised a belt with a 'snake' clasp, shoulder braces, bayonet frog, and entrenching tool helve carrier, tool head carrier, water bottle carrier, and two

large pouches each holding 50 rounds - the latter a reminder of the old Slade-Wallace equipment. The leather water bottle cover illustrated is not a typical example - the cloth covering was officially retained.

The Large pack ('valise') and haversack were of webbing with leather tabs. Up to 1918 some units could still be seen wearing this equipment in the trenches; where possible, webbing and leather sets were not mixed within one unit, but there were exceptions.

5 - The mess tin, originally carried inside the haversack, now increasingly appeared outside, in its drab cloth cover; the increased amounts of ammunition, grenades, and other items required in the trenches left no room for it in the pack. The D-section two-part mess tin changed little in basic design between the Napoleonic Wars and 1937.

6 - M1902 service dress trousers.

7 - Although it was strictly against regulations (and unsanitary!) to carry the **eating utensils** this way, it was often seen in period photographs.

8 - Khaki cloth puttees.

9 - Hobnailed Ammunition boots.

10 - SMLE rifle No 1 Mark III, .303 in. calibre.

11 - Breech cover, to protect the action of the rifle from rain and mud.

FRENCH INFANTRYMAN, VERDUN, 1916

The improvisations of autumn 1914, the terrible winter of 1914-15, and the partial and piecemeal issue of new horizon blue uniforms in spring 1915 left the French infantry with a very motley appearance. During the second half of 1915, a degree of standardisation was achieved; from that point on the front line infantryman, dressed from head to foot in the new uniform, began to resemble the theoretical image foreseen in the regulations of 9 December 1914. And a single new and essential element was added: the steel helmet. The French were the first to receive a general issue, which it was hoped would reduce the very high proportion of head wounds from bullets and shells; it was supplied to front line troops from September 1915. The definitive figure of the 'Poilu' had now been achieved: the soldier who would be tested by fire and steel in the holocaust of Verdun.

1 - M1915 Adrian pattern steel helmet. Its supply was an impressive feat, as more than three million were made and distributed before the end of 1915. Unfortunately, the protection it offered was inferior to that of the slightly later, and heavier, British and German models; the Adrian weighed only .765 kg and was made of mild steel. Its complex shape was copied from that worn by contemporary firemen; it comprised a shell, a two-part brim and a crest, with a pressed metal arm of service badge on the front. Issued with a blue grey paint finish, it was provided from late 1915 with a fabric cover in light blue or tan cloth.

2 - Blue cotton stock.

3 - M1914/15 greatcoat. At the end of 1915, to accommodate a further reserve of rifle rounds, a large reinforced pocket with a two-button flap was added to each side. This modification was made to existing coats, and there was often a contrast between the shades of cloth used; the illustrated coat is of a pale, imported fabric, but the added side pocket (just visible between gasmask and sidebag) and the backing to the insignia are of standard horizon blue, noticeably darker.

4 - The yellow arm-of-service **collar patches** briefly worn by infantry in the winter of 1914-15 were judged too visible; from May 1915 they were replaced by uniform cloth patches with dark blue pipings and numbers. This was also the colour selected for various rank and trade insignia. Our man is a young corporal of the 7th Infantry Regiment, his rank indicated by two short diagonal stripes on the forearms. The sleeve chevron indicating one-year's good conduct was introduced in April 1916.

5 - Canister, of grey-blue painted metal, for the TN gasmask and its associated goggles. This gas-mask, in its oval section canister, was issued from the end of 1915.

6 - Lebel rifle equipment. This had changed only in colour, natural leather being specified in the December 1914 regulations. The belt illustrated is of a simplified pattern with a single-prong buckle. The individual tool – here, M1915 wire cutters – is carried on the belt for ease of access.

7 - The simplified M1893/1914 **knapsack** of grey-green canvas supports spare shoes, the mess tin, tent accessories, the section's canvas bucket, and a private-purchase blanket in a black rubberised cover.

8 - Tan canvas M1892 sidebag.

9 - M1877 two-litre water bottle with horizon blue wool cover. This double-size water bottle was originally reserved for issue to troops in Africa, but it was extended to the whole army in Summer 1915. The cup hangs from a cork string.

10 - M1914 breeches/trousers. In April 1915 a yellow piping had been added to the outer seams, this is just visible in the rear view. Note the knee reinforcement patches to cater for the harsh conditions of trench warfare.

11 - Horizon blue cloth puttees.

12 - M1912 boots, 1916 modified, with side reinforcement rivet on the quarter.

13 - M1907/15 Berthier rifle, first model with angled bolt handle. Developed from the M1892 carbine, this was issued at the same time as the Lebel to make up required numbers. It was loaded with three-round charger clips of 8 mm cartridges. The M1907 sling was made in natural leather from the end of 1914.

GERMAN INFANTRYMAN, VERDUN, FEBRUARY 1916

The regulations of 21 September 1915 sanctioned various modifications carried out since the beginning of the war: the blackening of leather equipment, etc. and also introduced both a new greatcoat, and a new universal issue tunic, the 'Bluse'. Early in 1916 the useless Pickelhaube was replaced by an impressive and efficient steel helmet, which was first seen at Verdun. Now the German infantryman, too, had taken on the appearance which would be characteristic of the latter half of the war, very different from that of 1914. This austere, drab outfit would hardly change before the Armistice. The only touch of colour was provided by the bayonet knot, in distinctive colours identifying the soldier's company. This grenadier of the 184th Infantry carries assault equipment, his knapsack laid aside in favour of a lightened arrangement of immediately necessary items.

1 - M1916 'Stahhelm', hot-pressed from hardened silicon-nickel steel; more expensive than Allied helmets, which were cold-pressed, it was also heavier and gave better protection to the face, ears and neck. It had an efficient internal sizing system of leather tabs and pads, but retained the older M1891 Pickelhaube chin strap. Two external lugs allowed for fitting the 'Stirnpanzer,' a thick face armour for use by sentries and other exposed personnel. Although issued in a plain field grey finish, the helmet was sometimes camouflaged with paint or a cloth cover, the most common being of tan sandbag material.

2 - M1914 tunic. Our grenadier has not yet received the M1915 Bluse - in fact, all former tunic types including the M1907/10 were to be seen right through the war. In regulation style this tunic lacks cuff patches and simulated skirt pocket flaps. The white piping of the shoulder straps was now common for all line infantry; note the red embroidered '184' regimental numbers.

3 - M1915 Gummimaske, now carried in a grey painted metal box which gave better protection than the former canvas bag, but did not include a spare canister. The box was carried on a sling; the mask is placed here in the 'alert' position on the chest.

4 - M1915 assault pack, consisting of the M1915 greatcoat rolled in the M1892 tent section, the ends strapped together, and the roll arranged round the M1910 mess tin, here an enamelled war-time example. The breadbag's and various leather straps keep the pack together.

5 - M1887 breadbag, here an ersatz model in grey canvas, with a single attachment leather tab on the flap.

6 - M1907 water bottle, also an economy pattern in grey enamelled steel, covered with coarse and drab cloth.

7 - Individual tool, here the M1887 pick in its black leather carrier.

8 - Bayonet. Of wartime production, with grey painted steel hilt and scabbard. It is secured to the tool helve in the usual way to stop it flapping and clattering when the soldier was on the move. The 'Troddel' bayonet knot was still of the traditional pre-war type, the various coloured sections identifying the company according to a complex sequence: this combination is that of a 10th Company.

9 - M1895 belt. This, and one of the triple cartridge pouches, has been blackened as ordered in September 1915, the other has not. This kind of mixed equipment was not uncommon under front line conditions.

10 - M1914 trousers in stone grey; wartime examples often lacked the regulation red seam piping.

11 - M1866 boots in blackened leather.

12 - M1898 Mauser rifle, 7.92 mm calibre; the sling is another ersatz, of coarse canvas with leather tabs.

FRENCH CHASSEUR ALPIN, 1916

Alone within the French infantry arm of service, the 'Chasseurs' (light infantry) battalions were entirely garbed in dark blue in August 1914, and needed less urgent reforms than the red-trousered line infantrymen. They were also very attached to their special dress, which contributed to their fearsome reputation. Since the savage fighting in the Vosges mountains late in 1914, the Germans had christened them 'Black Devils', edited in the Chasseurs' lore to the more accurate 'Blue Devils'. Their dark blue uniform survived for a year and a half without major modification: the Chasseurs à Pied kept their blue képi, greatcoat and trousers with yellow pipings; and the Chasseurs Alpins (mountain infantry) retained until early 1916 their specific beret and tunic.

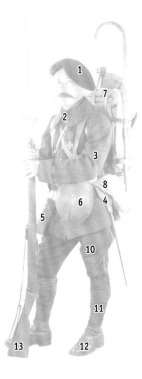

1 - M1889 beret for alpine troops, of traditional Basque pattern in very dark blue wool, with a bugle horn badge cut out of yellow cloth on the right front.

2 - Blue cotton stock.

3 - M1916 'Vareuse-dolman', in 'blued-iron grey' wool. Hardly modified since 1891, this modern-looking jacket had a very deep fall collar, two side pockets, and cuffs which could be folded down over the hands. It fastened with seven buttons embossed with the bugle. At the outbreak of war, the tunic was made of very dark blue, almost black, wool, with bright yellow unit numbers on the collar. The colour changed to this dark blue-grey in 1915, and from 12 November that year the collar patches featured less visible green pipings, unit number and bugle on uniform cloth. Until May 1916, crescent shaped pads designed to hold the equipment braces were sewn onto the shoulders. This corporal wears the 1915 abbreviated rank stripes in the green arm-of-service colour and has just been awarded the Croix de Guerre.

4 - M1915 Adrian helmet, painted blue-grey, with the Chasseurs' horn device in pressed steel.

5 - Oblong tin carrier for the M2 mask, blue-grey painted. It is suspended from one of the cartridge pouches. The M2 mask, associating goggles and a protective nose and mouth pad in one piece, was issued from spring 1916 until the beginning of 1918.

6 - Natural leather Lebel rifle equipment. The Y-shape of the M1888/1914 bayonet frog allowed its use with buttoned tabs on the tunic, a feature of French tunics and coats since the late 19th century. The theoretical ammunition issue for line infantry was four packets of eight rounds in each of the front pouches, and three packets in the rear pouch, giving a total of 88

rounds. Shortly before the war, the issue to Chasseurs was increased to 120 rounds.

7 - Alpine type pack, fashioned from the regular M1893/1914 knapsack, in grey-green canvas and natural leather. Note the curved handle 'Alpenstock' cane strapped to the left, and the cloak folded and stowed beneath the tent section on top of the pack. This is the hooded M1892 'Pélerine' of Alpine troops, fastened at the front by four small buttons. It was made in horizon blue from November 1915 onwards. The other elements of the pack are standard: the M1852 mess tin, the individual tool (here the bill-hook), and a section utensil (here the large 'bouteillon' dixie, its name corrupted from that of its inventor: Bouthéon).

8 - Canvas M1892 sidebag; this was seen in many different drab shades during the war.

9 - M1877 two-litre water bottle covered in grey-blue cloth; attached to one of the cork-strings is the cup, here an example covered with a dull grey-blue varnish.

10 - M1915 trousers in 'blued-iron grey' wool, a shade slightly darker and bluer than the jacket's, with yellow pipings. In August 1914 the Chasseurs wore straight trousers of the same colour, but at the beginning of 1915 they received the new pattern, tapered from the knee down.

11 - M1910 puttees in dark blue cloth. The Chasseurs Alpins had been the first to receive puttees in 1889, considered at the time both 'athletic and hygienic.'

12 - M1912/16 shoes in blackened leather.

13 - M1886/93 Lebel rifle, the needle bayonet features a cruciform section.

BRITISH INFANTRYMAN, SOMME OFFENSIVE, JULY 1916

T he battle of the Somme, which opened on 1 July 1916 with a major British attack, in fact lasted until 19 November that year, in a series of operations which would cost the Allied and German armies about 600,000 casualties each. The first day of the battle, however, has come to symbolise the sufferings of the British soldier. This was the first major offensive by Britain's 'New Army', largely composed of volunteers; their patriotic zeal matched, at least apparently, by a plan and resources which justified great confidence. Instead, 1 July 1916 turned out to be the costlier day in the British army's history: some 60,000 men were killed, wounded or taken prisoner within a few hours, for minimal gains. As to the infantryman's silhouette, two new elements are immediately noticeable: the steel 'shrapnel helmet,' and the system of coloured unit flashes on the uniform. Our figure wears the battle insignia of 'A' Company, 1st Battalion Lancashire Fusiliers.

1 - Mark 1 steel helmet, known as the 'Brodie' after its inventor. Manufactured from November 1915; by July 1916 a million had been delivered. The design offered protection against airbursts and shell fragments, and allowed easy mass production from Hadfield manganese steel. With the adoption of unit flashes on the uniform, such symbols were often painted on the helmet - here a representation of the yellow hackle traditionally worn on peacetime full dress headgear by the Lancashire Fusiliers.

2 - M1902 service tunic, as described previously. The red cloth triangle sewn to each sleeve identified the 29th Division, veterans of the Gallipoli campaign, who adopted it on arrival in France in March 1916. The various units of the division also wore patches in regimental colours on the back to assist quick unit identification in the attack (i.e. seen from the back). In the 1st Bn. Lancashire Fusiliers, the red and yellow were arranged in geometric patches identifying the companies. The need for quick identification had been recognised in the Boer War, when coloured flashes were sewn to helmet covers; the practice was reintroduced gradually and unevenly from mid-1915, but not all formations had adopted battle insignia by mid-1916.

The single chevron on each sleeve identifies a Lance-corporal, the most junior non-commissioned rank. The vertical gold bar sewn to the left forearm is a wound stripe, introduced in 1916. This regiment wore brass shoulder titles in the form of the fusiliers' flaming bomb over the initials 'LF'.

3 - M1908 webbing equipment, as described previously. This is the arrangement known as 'fighting order', with the haversack placed on the back and containing mess tin, eating utensils, shaving kit, a groundsheet, and two days' rations of bully beef and biscuits. Note that the lower set of three cartridge pouches are of the modified pattern introduced from October 1914,

with strap fasteners instead of press studs: when firing in the prone position or from trench parapets men reported that the original pattern easily came unfastened, with accidental loss of ammunition.

4 - Extra ammunition bandolier, a simple cotton container with five pockets each holding two five-round clips.

5 - Bag for the PH anti-gas hood.

6 - General service shovel. By now it was clear that assault troops had to have tools which allowed quick repair and consolidation of enemy trenches, so that they could withstand the almost inevitable artillery fire and counterattacks which the Germans were quick to unleash on any captured position. Picks, shovels, large wire cutters, empty sandbags, and even coils of barbed wire might add to the already heavy load of assault infantry.

7 - M1902 Service Dress trousers. A pattern unchanged for the whole war.

8 - Drab puttees.

9 - Hobnailed 'Ammunition boots'.

10 - No. I Mark III* service rifle, a slightly simplified version of the Mark III, introduced in 1916.

11 - M1908/13 bayonet, fixed for going 'over the top'. The 1913 modification involved deletion of the large quillon.

12 - M1908 webbing rifle sling.

13 - Wire cutters. These worked by pushing the rifle against a strand of wire caught between the cutter jaws.

ITALIAN ALPINE INFANTRYMAN, ITALIAN FRONT, 1916

Italy's northern frontiers lie through some of the most mountainous country in Europe. In October 1872 the Kingdom of Italy ordered the establishment of 15 experimental Alpine companies for defending the Alps. Created by Gen. Perruchetti, these 'Alpini' wore a number of special uniform and equipment items compatible with their missions. In 1906 the Alpini were the first Italian troops to experiment with uniforms of neutral colour, to blend into the grey, rocky terrain where they operated. The grey-green uniform was a success, and was extended to the whole army in 1909. Among Italy's best troops, the Alpini made great sacrifices during the fighting in the eastern Alps against the Austrians.

1 - M1910 hat, modelled after a traditional 19th century mountaineers hat, and adopted after an unsuccessful experiment with a melon-shaped headgear. This felt hat, which proved very popular, is still in use today. The frontal badge, embroidered in black, shows a bugle-horn with the regimental number in the centre and crossed rifles, the whole surmounted by a spread-winged eagle. On the left side was a tuft in battalion colour (white, red, green or blue respectively), and a black crow's-feather plume; the latter was white for senior officers, however.

2 - M1909 tunic. Single-breasted, with standing collar and fly front. The collar patches (bearing the Savoy star common to all Italian troops) were in green for this arm of service. The cuffs are pointed; on each shoulder a roll of cloth helped prevent equipment straps from slipping. Regulation tunics had no exterior pockets, and the side pockets visible on this example are a personal addition. There were two short rear vents with single button fastening. A field dressing was carried in an inside pocket.

3 - M1909 trousers, in the same grey-green colour as the tunic; these were straight cut, gathered at the ankles by tapes, and had two side pockets with slanted openings.

4 - Woollen socks. These were at first issued only to mountain troops, but were later extended to all infantry fighting in Northern Italy's mountains.

5 - M1909 puttees. Like the woollen stockings, these were originally peculiar to mountain troops but later issued more widely.

6 - M1912 ankle boots in brown leather, with a high top for support, and studded with climbing cleats. Again, this original Alpini item was extended to all infantry committed to the mountain front.

7 - M1907 equipment. Italy was alone among the belligerent nations in issuing leather equipment coloured to match the uniform. Il consisted of a belt with a single-prong buckle, a bayonet frog, a brace passing from the belt around the neck and down again, and two double cartridge pouches.

8 - M1891 bayonet in leather scabbard.

9 - M 1907 haversack, accommodating rations and small personal effects.

10 - M1907 water bottle, made of poplar or willow wood with iron strapping, and a leather tab for attaching to the belt or haversack.

11 - M1916 'Polivalente Z' gasmask, carried in a green-painted metal canister, although wood, or even cardboard were also used. A black-painted warning reads *'Anyone who loses his mask is risking death; keep it with you al all times'.*

12 - M1891 Mannlicher-Carcano rifle, 6.5 mm calibre.

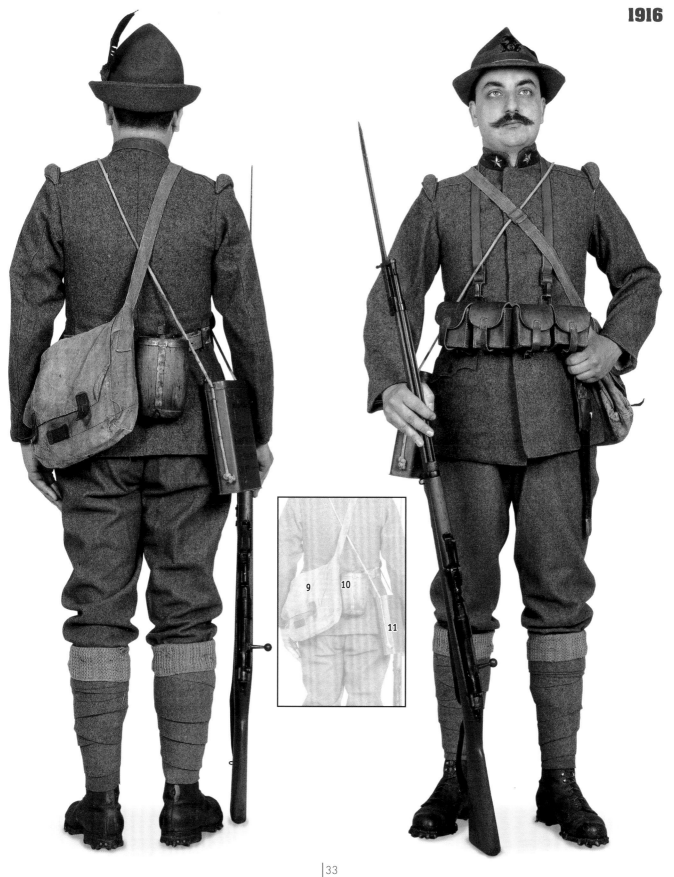

9 10

11

RUSSIAN INFANTRYMAN, EASTERN FRONT, WINTER 1916

For winter campaigning the Russian soldier was issued with the same basic uniform as for summer, but in a heavier woollen cloth. Over this was worn a heavy, generously cut greatcoat, and a fur or fleece cap. But centuries-long experience of extremely cold weather prompted various improvisations. Furthermore, the problems of supplying a huge army spread along a vast front were never solved with any consistency by the Imperial Russian command. The plight, and the morale, of the 'frontovik' steadily declined under the terrible conditions, and the gap between officers and men widened. This eventually led to the 1917 mutinies, to the replacement of the Imperial regime by the Kerenski government and to the seizure of power by the Bolsheviks. In March 1918 the latter signed a peace treaty at Brest-Litovsk, thus releasing large German forces to reinforce those on the Western Front.

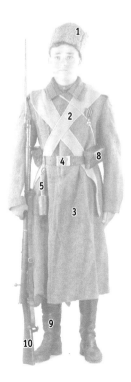

1 - M1910 sheepskin cap, or 'Papakha', issued in either natural or artificial fleece, with a greenish-khaki cotton top. The band could be turned down to protect the neck and ears. The stamped metal orange and black cockade was pinned to the front, as on the visored summer cap.

2 - The 'Bashlyk' was a traditional Russian item, best described as a hood with long tails, made in thick tan wool. Its use was only officially allowed when the temperature sank to - 80 C. It is worn here thrown back; when raised, the hood completely covered the head (including the headgear) and neck. Its tails are crossed at the front and tucked under the belt; when the hood was raised they were knotted.

3 - M1881 greatcoat, still worn by many Russian troops despite the introduction of a new pattern in 1911. In fact it was superior for very cold weather, having a double-breasted front fastened by hooks, while the M1911 was single-breasted and bore very visible brass buttons. In 1917 the older style was officially reintroduced. Of grey-brown wool, it had a two-button half-belt at the rear, which was deeply pleated. The collar patches were in arm-of-service colours, here the infantry's raspberry red, as were the broad shoulder straps bearing a regimental monogram or number. This soldier's decoration is the St. George's Cross for

other ranks on its orange and black ribbon, the colours of the Romanov dynasty.

4 - Riflemen wore blackened **leather belts,** here with the M1904 brass plate stamped with the Imperial eagle.

5 - 'Stick' hand grenade.

6 - 'Linnemann' pattern entrenching tool in a cloth carrier. This was the typical tool issued to Russian troops.

7 - 'Zelinski' pattern gasmask, carried in a narrow metal box painted green.

8 - M1893 brown leather cartridge pouches, each holding six charger clips of five rounds; another 40 rounds were normally carried in the haversack.

9 - Blackened leather boots of standard pattern. Shortages dictated the increasing issue of ankle boots and puttees in place of the traditional boots.

10 - M1891 '3-line' Mosin Nagant rifle of 7.62 mm calibre. The M1891 permanently fixed bayonet was an archaic design with a socket fitting and flattened tip.

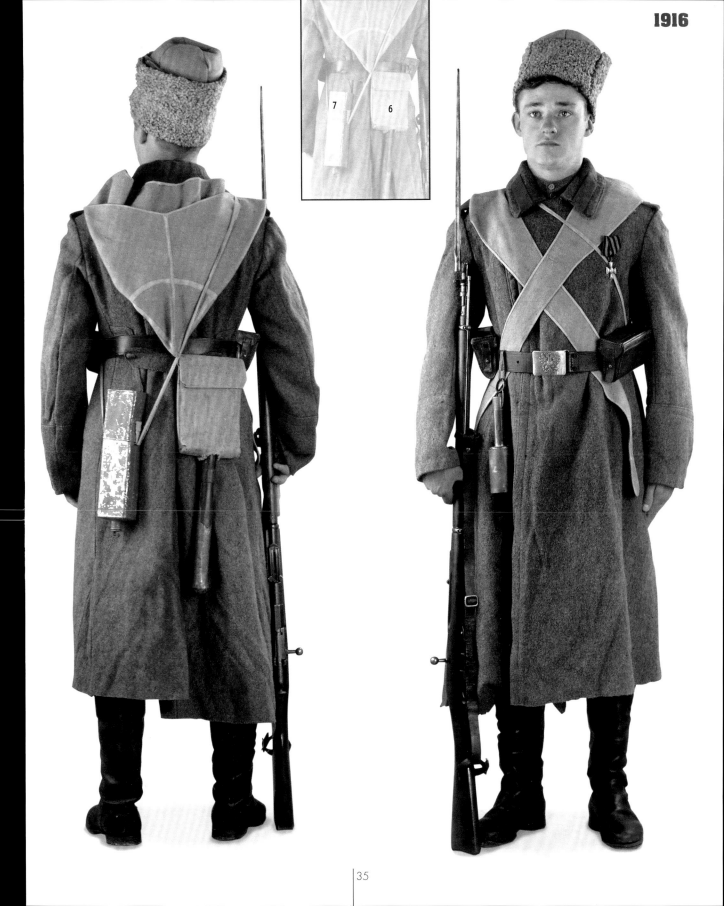

7   6

FRENCH FOREIGN LEGIONNAIRE, 1916

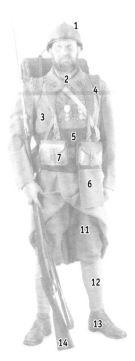

From the first days of the war a constant stream of foreign volunteers allowed the creation of four 'march regiments' of the famous Foreign Legion, bolstered by veterans from the North African garrisons. These units were dressed in the line infantry uniform, with very few distinctive insignia. As of spring 1915, like the rest of the infantry, the Foreign Legion was garbed in horizon blue. 1915 also saw a decrease in strength, due both to very heavy battle casualties and to the release of large contingents of Belgian, Italian and Russian volunteers to their national armies. In October, Legion units remaining on the Western Front were reorganised into a single 'march regiment', the RMLE. During the winter of 1915/16 their horizon blue uniforms were replaced by the mustard-coloured equivalent prescribed for all 'African' troops. The RMLE covered itself with glory and shared with the RICM ('Régiment d'infanterie coloniale du Maroc') the honour of being the most heavily decorated regiment of the war.

1 - M1915 steel helmet. Issued in a grey-blue finish, this was repainted khaki in 1916 to match the new uniform. The Legion did not have a distinctive helmet badge, displaying the infantry grenade, and 'RF' initials.

2 - Khaki cotton stock.

3 - M1915 greatcoat in mustard-coloured wool. In August 1915, after a crisis in uniform supply, the War Ministry decided to stop production of the simplified M1914 coat and to reintroduce a double-breasted pattern. The large fall collar and the two cartridge pockets on the sides were retained; otherwise the coat returned to the M1877 design, with two rows of six buttons, and false cuffs with a buttoned rear slit. This coat, also made in horizon blue, was issued to units from Africa in winter 1915/16. The only distinguishing marks were the collar patches bearing two pipings and the traditional grenade badge, in the green colour assigned to the Legion under the 9 December 1914 regulations. Until the beginning of 1917 the collar patches were rectangular.

4 - Unit citation lanyard or 'Fourragère', introduced in April 1916. For two or three mentions in Army despatches, units received this in the green and red of the Croix de Guerre ribbon. The RMLE was thus honoured on 5 June 1916, and wore this lanyard for a year. Our légionnaire, a veteran of colonial campaigns, wears three individual awards: the Médaille Militaire, Croix de Guerre and Médaille Coloniale.

5 - Blue woollen cholera-belt, 4.2 m (more than 13 ft.) long. This was typical of units from Africa, providing warmth on cold desert nights and back support for heavily laden men on long marches. It was blue for the Zouaves and Foreign Legion; on parade it was worn visibly, over the coat and under the belt equipment.

6 - Box for the M2 gas mask, here painted in brown.

7 - Lebel rifle equipment in the new natural leather version: M1903/14 belt, M1892/1914 braces and three M1916 pouches.

8 - Knapsack. This is the same as on pp. 24-25, with the substitution of the section-sized dixie ('Bouteillon'), here of a simplified wartime pattern without a handle on the cover, and a nonreflective greyish finish.

9 - M1892 sidebag in light brown canvas.

10 - M1877 two-litre water bottle with brown cloth cover. Per regulations, it was supposed to be slung with the smaller spout forward.

11- M1914 trousers, of exactly the same cut as the horizon blue trousers worn by the Metropolitan infantry. This featured in theory the infantry yellow seam piping, but under the conditions of wartime manufacture this was often omitted.

12 - Puttees. The mustard brown shade used for these uniforms was unstable, and one man might display a variety of tones on the various items of his uniform. As a rule, the French-made fabric was of a yellower shade than the browner material imported from Britain.

13 - M1912 shoes, modified 1916.

14 - M1907/15 rifle, 8 mm calibre, known as the Berthier; here, the second pattern with a straight bolt handle. It is fitted with an M1915 bayonet, without quillon.

BELGIAN INFANTRYMAN, WESTERN FRONT, 1917

As illustrated and described on pp. 4-5, the uniform and equipment issued to the Belgian infantryman at the outbreak of the Great War were completely unsuitable for modern warfare. From the first battles of August 1914 it was clear that the archaic shako and front cartridge pouch needed to be replaced, and that the pack was too heavy. At the end of 1914, the infantry fighting on the Yser received a simplified outfit, but this was purely transitional while completely new uniforms and equipment were prepared. The new appearance of the Belgian infantryman was settled in February 1915. It was clearly inspired partly by that of the French soldier, as both the helmet and the gasmask were supplied by France. The uniform was made of brown serge procured from Britain, however; as well as the equipment, very similar to the British M1908 pattern.

1 - M1915 steel helmet, painted brown; this was the Adrian, exactly as issued to French troops, apart from the Belgian army lion's head badge.

2 - Cotton stock, brown in colour, worn to protect the neck from chafing against the tunic collar.

3 - M1915 greatcoat, double-breasted and fastened by two rows of four buttons painted brown and bearing a lion motif. It had two large side pockets with straight buttoned flaps. The large falling collar bore no insignia; the arm-of-service was indicated by the shoulder strap piping, here yellow for the Carabiniers. There was an integral half-belt on the back, over two vertical pockets. Two buttons allowed the skirts to be fastened up on the march.

4 - M1915 tunic in brown serge, worn under the greatcoat. This single-breasted garment had a standing collar with rounded tips, and bore green collar patches piped in yellow for the Carabiniers.

5 - M1915 webbing equipment. At first glance very similar to the British M1908 pattern, it actually varied in many details. It consisted of two four-pocket cartridge pouch sets, arranged one-over-three on each side, each holding two five-round clips of 7.65 mm ammunition, giving 80 rounds in all. Shoulder braces with a hook-buckle system at the front were connected to the top of the cartridge carriers and with both the top

and bottom of the knapsack. The latter featured five sets of straps for the tent section, blanket and mess tin. The haversack hung from the right side; on the left, the bayonet frog, and a Linnemann entrenching tool reversed in a web carrier with the water bottle hanging over it. The bottle was of aluminium, covered in brown cloth and suspended in a web carrier. Like the British set, this equipment could be set up in various ways and could be donned or discarded in one piece, like a jacket, by fastening and unfastening the belt. The M1915 equipment, however, was very expensive and only issued in large numbers at the end of the war.

6 - The M1914 mess tin in aluminium was now painted in brown.

7 - French LTN gasmask, in its brown metal canister.

8 - M1915 trousers in brown serge; these were straight-cut, with two slash side pockets, and a half-belt for adjustment at the rear.

9 - Brown leather gaiters, identical apart from their colour to the peacetime model; they laced up the front by means of hooks.

10 - Standard ankle boots.

11 - M1889 Mauser carbine, calibre 7.65 mm.

1916

6 5

5

39

ITALIAN INFANTRYMAN, ITALY, MARCH 1917

The Italian army was committed to the Great War on the side of the Allies, rather than that of the Central Powers, largely due to British diplomacy. The 1882 Triple Alliance with Germany and Austria-Hungary had been prompted largely by colonial rivalry with France; and Austria-Hungary – Italy's former imperial ruler – could never be a natural ally, especially given Austro-Hungarian delay in meeting Italian demands over border territories. Thus on 23 May 1915, Italy declared war on the Central powers. The M1909 grey-green uniform was of modern cut, and was retained with only minor changes to collar and pockets right up until the end of the Second World War. The appearance of the Italian infantryman would change little over the next two years, apart from the adoption of two vital items: the steel helmet and gasmask. It was in the outfit illustrated that the Italian infantryman went into the indecisive offensive of spring 1917 on the eastern front, the 'Tenth Battle of the Isonzo', whose title sums up the costly futility of these operations.

1 - M1916 steel helmet. Derived from the French design but stamped in one piece. The arm of service badge and unit number were sometimes painted on the front. The factory finish was a dark grey-green.

2 - Grey-green helmet cover, worn to prevent reflection. A wide variety was used, differing in material and details. The badge was often embroidered or sewn to the front.

3 - Metal eye-protectors, with narrow horizontal slits; these were intended to protect against shell splinters.

4 - M1909 grey-green universal issue tunic. The standing collar bore distinctive patches. In the line infantry these identified the brigade: the green and red example illustrated was that of the Cremona Brigade, comprising the 21st and 22nd Infantry Regiments. Like all such patches it bears the star of Savoy.

5 - M1907 leather equipment, as illustrated and described on pages 20 and 32.

6 - M1907 ammunition pouches. Each of the two pockets in each pouch held four charger clips each of six cartridges, giving the rifleman a basic load of 96 rounds.

7 - The individual tool here is a hatchet in an M1891 carrier, which also allows the attachment of the M1891 bayonet in its leather scabbard.

8 - M1907 haversack, in canvas with leather straps; it had external loops allowing the attachment of various items, including the water bottle. This pack was the single most important item of the Italian soldier's gear, since it could be rigged either as a knapsack or as a slung haversack, and accommodated his rations and small personal effects.

9 - M1909 water bottle, of old-fashioned 'keg' design made of poplar or willow wood; it was encased in a leather carrier for either the belt or haversack.

10 - M1916 'Polivalente Z' gasmask, this example is carried in a green-painted metal canister but it was often seen with a container of wood or cardboard. The stencilled warning reminded the soldier to keep it handy at all times.

11 - M1909 trousers, straight-cut in the same cloth as the tunic, and tightened at the ankle with tapes. There were two slanted side pockets.

12 - Woollen stockings were non-regulation, but tolerated from 1916 onwards.

13 - M1909 puttees in grey-green cloth. Originally for the Alpini, these were issued to the whole army when Italy entered the war.

14 - M1912 brown leather ankle boots. Also intended for the mountain troops, they were studded with heavy hobnails and cleats. When the bulk of the Italian infantry was committed to mountain fighting the boots were issued on a wider basis.

15 - M1891 Mannlicher-Carcano rifle, 6.5 mm calibre: the standard arm of the Italian army.

8

9   10

AUSTRIAN STURMTRUPPEN, ITALIAN FRONT, 1917

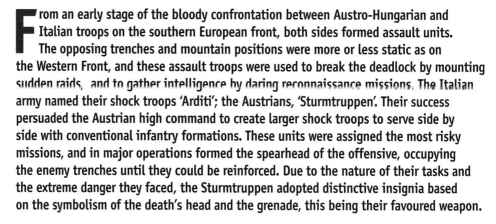

From an early stage of the bloody confrontation between Austro-Hungarian and Italian troops on the southern European front, both sides formed assault units. The opposing trenches and mountain positions were more or less static as on the Western Front, and these assault troops were used to break the deadlock by mounting sudden raids, and to gather intelligence by daring reconnaissance missions. The Italian army named their shock troops 'Arditi'; the Austrians, 'Sturmtruppen'. Their success persuaded the Austrian high command to create larger shock troops to serve side by side with conventional infantry formations. These units were assigned the most risky missions, and in major operations formed the spearhead of the offensive, occupying the enemy trenches until they could be reinforced. Due to the nature of their tasks and the extreme danger they faced, the Sturmtruppen adopted distinctive insignia based on the symbolism of the death's head and the grenade, this being their favoured weapon.

1 - M1917 Austrian steel helmet, very similar to the German pattern, apart from the fabric chinstrap, the light brown finish and the rivet set higher on the shell.

2 - M1916 tunic in 'nettle green' cloth. This replaced the M1909 'pike grey' model and was simplified in many details for wartime manufacture. It had a soft stand-and fall collar, five apparent front buttons, and four front pockets with box pleats and scalloped flaps. Many variations of cloth and colour are known, including field grey, a yellowish brown, and even 'grigio-verde' examples made from captured Italian material. This trooper wears on his collar two six-point stars, made of bone or celluloid, for the rank of first class private.

3 - M1915 gasmask, an Austrian version of the German Gummimaske; the green-painted metal canister had a sling of drab fabric.

4 - Brown leather belt with brass plate bearing the Imperial Austro-Hungarian double headed eagle. As the war progressed an ersatz grey-painted iron plate became most common.

5- M1895 cartridge pouches in brown leather. Each of the four pouches held two five-round charger clips of 8-mm ammunition, giving 40 rounds in all. Variants in substitute materials, such as canvas, are known.

6 - Skull-crusher trench club, a typical weapon for these raiding units who often fought hand-to-hand. A very wide variety were improvised, usually with a heavy lead-weighted head on a wooden handle.

7 - Trench knives were equally common among

the Sturmtruppen. Again, there were many improvised patterns, but this is the regulation M1917 issue, with a wooden grip and a double-edged blade, carried in a metal scabbard painted green or brown, and fixed to the belt by a leather or cloth tab.

8 - 'Tyrolean' rucksack. This gradually replaced the rigid horsehide knapsack from 1916 onwards. Practical, comfortable and roomy, it was made in strong green or brown canvas. The broad straps had front braces which hooked to rings on the back of the ammunition pouches.

9 - Austrian version of the German breadbag, in green or brown canvas. This could be slung round the body or attached to the belt with loops and hooks. The interior was divided into compartments for the water bottle, mess tin and rations.

10 - Trench periscope: a simple metal tube with mirrors, painted matt green.

11 - M1907 enamelled water bottle. Although normally carried inside the knapsack, it could be hung externally.

12 - M1917 trousers in nettle green wool; these had two tightening buttons below the knee. They were later replaced by the mountain troops' semi-breeches.

13 - Puttees, made of many varieties and shades of cloth.

14 - Brown leather ankle boots, standard pattern.

15 - M1895 Steyr-Mannlicher rifle, 8-mm calibre, with M1895 bayonet.

ITALIAN ASSAULT TROOPER, ITALIAN FRONT, 1917

From the beginning of the war on this southern European front, the difficulties of the mountain terrain and the solid Austro-Hungarian defences imposed several problems on the Italian army. Especially in the north-western sector, the prospect of mounting major offensives was daunting: the difficulty of assembling and moving up men and large amounts of matériel, and the exposure of all but stealthy movements to artillery observers on higher ground, more or less confined tactics to small-scale raids and patrols. Consequently, special assault groups were formed to carry out these tasks and in time, such units were incorporated within infantry battalions. These 'Arditi' ('bold ones') also had a mission in conventional offensive operations, when they were committed to seizing key enemy positions. In 1917 these groups were reorganised by one Captain Barri, receiving peculiar uniforms and equipment items. These forerunners of the modern special forces faced extraordinary hazards, and earned a unique reputation in the Italian army.

1 - M1916 Italian helmet. See also on p. 40. As in other armies at the time, helmets were generally worn with antireflective cloth covers of drab shades. This gray cloth cover is faded from exposure to the weather.

2 - M1909 tunic in grey-green cloth, a design similar to that issued to the Bersaglieri bicycle troops. It had an open collar, here bearing black patches for the Arditi, who upheld the traditions of the Venetian Republic's Carbonari. Breast pockets were made both with and without pleats, and with single-button flaps. A large poacher's pocket was provided at the back, to hold Thévenot explosive charges. Three large front buttons were concealed by a fly and there were two buttoned belt loops. The left sleeve is adorned with the arm-of-service badge, a sword wreathed with laurels or oak leaves, embroidered in black on a grey-green backing.

3 - Regulation woollen sweater, grey-green in colour and with a roll neck; it was modelled on a type issued to the Alpini.

4 - M1909 trousers, similar to those worn by the Alpini but more generously cut in the thigh to give greater ease of movement.

5 - Woollen hose; again borrowed from the moun-

tain troops, these were considered more practical than puttees.

6 - M1912 brown leather ankle-high boots, studded with climbing nails and cleats.

7 - M1907 leather equipment. This was reduced to the minimum for the Arditi's special missions: the belt and a single ammunition pouch, the weight being supported by the tunic belt loops.

8 - The all-purpose M1907 haversack, used in the assault to carry quantities of hand grenades.

9 - M1916 'Polivalente Z' gasmask in its painted metal container.

10 - Water bottle. The new pattern was made of aluminium covered with grey-green cloth, and hung from the belt by a strap. Among the Arditi, it more frequently held brandy than water.

11 - Fighting knife, here the regulation issue, although improvised knives and clubs for hand-to-hand combat were often seen. This type was fashioned from an M1870 Vetterli bayonet, with wooden grips, and its blackened leather scabbard.

8 10

9

FRENCH TRENCH RAIDER, SUMMER 1917

The reform of French uniforms achieved under the difficult conditions of 1914 and 1915 had monopolised the efforts of the high command, and no comparable reform of the soldier's equipment had taken place. Unfortunately, an improvement approved in 1913 – the replacement of the haversack and water bottle straps by belt attachments – had been forgotten in the turmoil. All in all, the regulation equipment of the French infantryman remained almost unchanged throughout the war from that worn at the end of the previous century. Cumbersome and uncomfortable on the march, the full knapsack order was simply impossible for troops going into the assault. Consequently the high command eventually authorised a lightened 'assault order' for men going over the top.

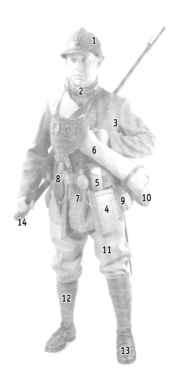

1 - M1915 steel helmet. interestingly, from summer 1916 onwards helmet covers were abolished on the grounds that filthy scraps of cloth were being carried into head wounds, with serious infection risks. Stocks of dull grey-blue paint were issued for whole units to repaint their helmets in the field, and new helmets were finished in this way at the factory. Our trench raider has chosen an uncommon solution in the French army: splashes of brown, green and ochre paint over the grey-blue finish in an attempt at camouflage.

2 - Blue cotton stock.

3 - M1914/15 tunic. Although issued to each soldier, this was seen usually as a barracks and walking out garment. The greatcoat remained the regular battle garment and the tunic was only worn under it in very cold weather. On rare occasions, however, the tunic was worn alone during summer operations. It had a standing collar fastened by a hook-and-eye, five small buttons down the front; cuffs and shoulders were plain. There were two side pockets, and on the left side a single buttoned belt loop. The collar patches are for the 51st Infantry Regiment. The additional coloured disc, introduced in July 1916, identified the battalion (here, yellow for the 3rd). On the left upper sleeve are three service chevrons (the first for 12 months' service, and another for every additional six months' period). The flaming grenade badge is that of assault grenadiers. The large white patch sewn to the back helped commanders to keep track of the progress of the assault through their binoculars.

4 - M2 gas mask in the 'alert' position; its canister hangs in the usual position below the left hand cartridge carrier.

5 - Lebel rifle equipment in brown leather, the belt is the simplified pattern with single-pronged buckle.

6 - Assault pack. The knapsack was left in the trench, and a horseshoe roll was made up with the blanket and tent section. The tent pegs and cords were not carried; they were useless in the line, where the tent section was used as an all-purpose groundsheet or overhead cover. The roll was strapped together at the ends; another strap often secured a bundle of sandbags, to help fortify a shell hole if the squad was pinned down.

7 - Fighting knife, here the M1915 made by cutting down an M1886 bayonet and fitting it with a wooden grip and leather scabbard.

8 - Entrenching tools were slipped under the belt; here, the M1909 Seurre pattern pick-spade. Other troops might carry M1916 general service picks and shovels with removable helves shortened for ease of carrying.

9 - Two M1892 sidebags; one contained rations, the other grenades and signalling equipment. An OF1916 grenade is also clipped to the belt.

10 - Two two-litre water bottles. The difficulty of supplying drinking water to men in combat was considerable, and had prompted the introduction of the double-sized water bottle in 1915. In the assault one bottle typically contained wine mixed with water, the other coffee laced with cheap rum.

11 - M1914 trousers in horizon blue wool (note the different blue shades over the uniform components) with yellow seam piping for the infantry.

12 - Puttees in light grey-blue cloth.

13 - M1912 service shoes, modified 1916.

14 - M1907/15 Berthier rifle, carried slung by this grenadier.

RUSSIAN INFANTRYMAN, FRANCE, 1917

To provide a visible demonstration of inter-Allied solidarity, Csar Nicholas II agreed, at the urging of President Poincaré, to send an expeditionary corps on the Western Front. The men who made up these two brigades were handpicked; all could read and write and met the recruiting standards for the Imperial Guard. All the officers were fluent in French. The uniforms and insignia were Russian, but the equipment and weapons were provided by the French in order to alleviate supply problems, particularly of ammunition. The Russian Expeditionary Corps was commanded first by General Palitzine, and subsequently by General Zankeleievitch; it fought with distinction until the 1917 revolution in the motherland and the murderous losses sustained during the Nivelle offensive sapped its morale. The Russian corps was withdrawn from France in 1918.

1 - M1915 French helmet. Russia did not manufacture a national pattern during the war. The two million examples provided to Russia were distinguished by a double-headed eagle badge, and were painted brown. This helmet was issued to the Russian expeditionary corps in France and in Macedonia.

2 - Gymnastierka M1912 shirt-tunic in summer weight cotton, the standing collar fastened (here, at the front) by two small buttons. This pullover garment had a buttoned vent to mid-chest. The examples issued to the expeditionary corps were made both in Russia and in France. The only insignia were the large, stiff shoulder boards, which for the expeditionary corps were brown, sometimes piped in white. The chest badge is that of a 3rd class marksman; note how it is attached to the leather brace.

3 - Russian M1914 belt in brown leather, much narrower than the old type with a plate, and fastened by a single-prong buckle.

4 - French M1892/1914 shoulder braces in brown leather, a Y-strap arrangement which hooked to rings mounted on the rear of each of the cartridge pouches.

5 - French M1905/14 (or M1916) ammunition pouches in brown leather; the front pair each held 10 charger-clips of three 8-mm cartridges, the rear one eight clips, giving a total of 84 rounds for men armed with the M1907/15 Berthier rifle.

6 - French M1892 sidebag, containing rations.

7 - French M1877 two-litre water bottle in tinned iron, covered with reclaimed horizon blue cloth, with the usual cup attached to one of the cork stopper cords.

8 - Russian M1910 knapsack, made of a proofed grey-beige canvas and with leather flap tabs. This contained changes of clothing and additional ammunition. Its long, wide strap enabled it to be slung, or worn on the back.

9 - French M2 gas mask in its blue-painted metal canister; some were painted brown to match the uniform.

10 - M1907 semi-breeches, in cotton or wool depending on the season. Loose in the thigh, they tapered to the knee in order to tuck easily into the boots. There were two slash side pockets. Like all the uniform items issued to the expeditionary corps they might be made in Russia, in France of French material, or in France of Russian material, as here is the case.

11 - Blackened leather boots.

12 - M1907/15 Berthier rifle, 8-mm calibre, as issued to all personnel of the two brigades apart from the machine gunners, whose personal weapon was the M1892 carbine.

13 - French M1915 bayonet, without quillon.

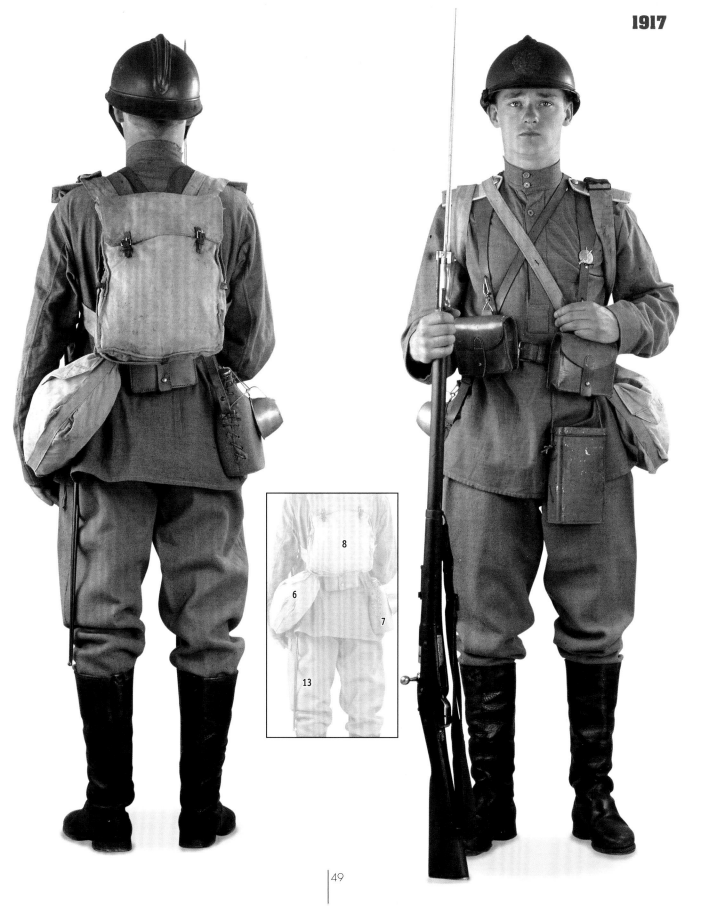

UNITED STATES INFANTRYMAN, JUNE 1917

The entry into the war of the United States in 1917 was the decisive event which made Allied victory certain. The nation's vast population and extensive industrial base allowed her to transform a small peacetime army of 200,000 men into a force of more than three million in record time. The powerful American Expeditionary Force added decisively to the Allies' resources in the last phase of the war, which had already dragged on for three years. The first 'doughboys' to come ashore at St. Nazaire in June 1917 made an immediate impression, as much by their fitness and enthusiasm as by their modern uniforms and equipment. Since the Spanish-American War at the turn of the century, the USA had procured drab uniforms, and combat equipment was in the canvas duck and cotton webbing patterned by Capt. Anson Mills. This soldier of the 28th Infantry , 1st Division carries the full marching order as he disembarks with the first contingents.

1 - M1912 campaign hat in rabbit fur felt, its crown shaped in the 'Montana peak' style and pierced by four ventilation eyelets. There was a leather sweatband inside, and a practical leather chin strap. The cords, ending in a slider and acorns at the front, were in arm-of-service colours for the enlisted ranks: here the infantry's light blue.

2 - M1912 tunic in 'Olive drab' wool, with a standing collar and four patch pockets with pointed flaps. The five large front buttons and four smaUnited States seal. Dulled bronze collar discs bore the 'US' cypher on the right side and the branch of service emblem on the left. Here, the crossed rifles of the infantry, with the regimental number above and the company letter below.

3 - M1912 semi-breeches, tapered to fit into the leggings and reinforced at the knees. These had two slanted front pockets, two hip pockets, and a right front fob pocket. Infantrymen received them with loops at the waist for a fabric belt.

4 - M1910 rifle belt for dismounted troops; each of the ten pockets held two five-round charger clips, giving a total of 100 rounds. On early belts, the flaps fastened with press studs bearing the American eagle.

5 - M1910 pouch for the First aid packet, closed by two plain press studs.

6 - M1910 water bottle with its cup, which fitted over the bottom of the former. Both were stored in a fabric carrier lined with felt, that closed by two tabs with press studs.

7 - M1910 haversack and 'Pack carrier' (bottom part), the combination worn for the march. The haversack, with two front straps and a short tab at the rear which hooked to the belt, contained rations, washing kit, and (in the outer pouch) mess tin. The M1905 bayonet was hooked to the left in its M1910 fabric and leather scabbard; and the M1910 shovel in its carrier under the mess tin pouch. The awkwardly long 'Pack carrier' accommodated changes of clothing, blankets, groundsheet/poncho, tent section and accessories. The disadvantages of this pack, although modern for its day, were that it was complicated to assemble; could not be worn without the belt and – worst of all – would only accommodate the regulation load, and no extra front line necessities.

8 - M1910 canvas leggings, laced through eyelets at the front.

9 - M1904 'marching shoes' in russet brown leather. Although comfortable for dry weather, they were inadequate in the sodden trenches of France.

10 - Springfield M1903/15 rifle in .30-06 calibre, with M1907 sling. This excellent bolt-action rifle, generally based on the Mauser design, served on well into World War II.

GERMAN ASSAULT TROOPER, WESTERN FRONT, 1918

Like the Italians and the Austrians, the German army formed assault units for raiding and for spearheading attacks. The 'Sturm' battalions, organised within each field army, contained not only infantrymen but many specialists: assault gunners with light cannon, machine gunners, trench mortar crews, and sappers armed with flame-throwers. The men carried full-sized tools rather than the mere individual entrenching tools, enabling them to dig in quickly and consolidate captured positions while awaiting reinforcement by the conventional infantry. The favoured weapons included trench knives, clubs and spades sharpened into hatchets, and especially a large number of grenades. This type of unit called for a radical change in tactics: a concentration on rigidly-scheduled, small-scale attacks on specific targets rather than the large frontal assaults which had invited such murderous losses. Warfare had truly become a trade for professionals.

1 - M1918 steel helmet, differing from the M1916 by its new, improved chin strap and attachments. In the last weeks of the war a parallel type appeared, with cut-outs on the rim at each side to reduce the 'echo chamber' effect of the bell-shaped shell.

2 - M1915 'Bluse'. The new tunic intended to replace the M1907/10 and M1914 (although both continued to be seen). This was cut from dark field grey cloth, with a fall collar faced with green. The six large front buttons were concealed by a fly; and it had two slanted, flapped side pockets. The shoulder straps were narrower and detachable; nevertheless they were often sewn firmly down to prevent snagging. They were piped, in white for infantry, and bore the regimental number or monogram in red. The 1915 tunic was of the same design for the whole army, though made in a greener shade for the light Infantry and rifles (Jäger and Schützen).

3 - Rifle ammunition bandolier ('Patronen-Tragegurte') in drab light grey cloth, its ten pockets holding a total of 14 five-round clips (70 rounds).

4 - Two sandbags, slung like water wings and holding various grenades. These were popular among assault troops.

5 - M1895 belt in blackened leather, here with an M1915 grey-painted Prussian belt plate.

6 - M1915 stick grenade.

7 - M1822 general service spade, carried in a cloth case reinforced with leather, the helve being secured to a shoulder strap by a short leather tab or thong.

8 - M1917 'Lederschutzmaske' gasmask, in waterproofed leather with a filter canister. Its grey-painted metal case was slung from a fabric strap.

9 - Trench knife, as carried by most assault troops.

10 - Grey cloth bag for a spare gasmask canister, hanging from the belt.

11 - Mauser Kar 98a carbine, 7.92 mm calibre, as issued to assault units. It was carried slung, to free the hands during the attack.

12 - M1917 trousers in field grey cloth, reintroducing this colour which had been abandoned in 1914. By this stage of the war army cloth was eaked out with ersatz fibres (such as nettle) for economic reasons and therefore of poor quality. The Sturmtruppen also used stocks of the mountain troops' special trousers. Elbows and knees were often reinforced with leather patches.

13 - Puttees, now made out of indifferent material, German or Allied, in a wide range of drab shades.

14 - M1901 ankle boots in brown leather, laced up with eyelets and hooks.

1918

8

7

10

11

U.S. INFANTRYMAN, WESTERN FRONT, SUMMER 1918

After a period of training with the French, the 'Doughboys' discovered the reality of trench warfare, which had worn down both their allies and enemies. They also quickly acquired those necessary items which had not been provided by the US Army. At first the steel helmet and gasmask ('small box respirator') were supplied by the British, even though they were subsequently manufactured in America. Other items included tools of different kinds and trench knives. After a few months of fighting, puttees and sturdier boots became widespread. The American infantryman now looked very similar to his British comrades; but he was still distinguished by a fresh, aggressive attitude, which would not be found wanting when it was tested to the limit during the great German offensive of 1918.

1 - M1917 steel helmet, copied from the British 1916 pattern which had been supplied initially to the American Expeditionary Force. It was made of manganese steel and painted nonreflective green-brown. The lining was in black patent leather and the chin strap in brown leather.

2 - M1918 tunic in olive drab wool. This simplified pattern had inside hanging pockets, only the flaps remaining visible. Each of the chevrons on the left forearm indicates six months' overseas service.

3 - M1917 gasmask, also patterned after the British issue, comprising a rubberised cloth face piece connected by a corrugated rubber tube to the filter canister carried permanently in the canvas carrier, here slung on the chest in the 'alert' position.

4 - M1917 cartridge belt, its ten pockets containing a total of 100 rounds. They were closed by an improved press stud system, the 'lift-the-dot' type.

5 - M1917 trench knife, with a wooden grip, a knuckleduster hand guard and a strong triangular-section blade. Like many items of equipment, it was attached to eyelets along the bottom of the belt by a brass hook.

6 - M1910 canteen and cup assembly, carried in a felt-lined fabric pouch fastened by two tabs and press studs.

7 - Rifle ammunition bandolier in light brown cotton, slung by means of a tape whose length was simply adjusted by a knot. Each of the five pockets held two five-round charger clips of .30-06 ammunition. Again copied directly from the British equivalent, these bandoliers were issued fully loaded.

8 - M1912 olive drab semi-breeches, tapered at the knees and calves. These remained unchanged during the war.

9 - Puttees in an olive drab shade close to that of the uniform. They were rapidly adopted after the AEF had had a taste of trench warfare. The laced canvas leggings, which looked neat and strong, were in fact too complex and fragile for the rigours of the front line, and were quickly abandoned.

10 - M1917 service shoes, in thick brown hide; these were much more serviceable than the M1904 russet marching shoes they replaced, and which had proved inadequate in the constant wet of the trenches. These were relegated to use for walking-out and parades behind the lines.

11 - M1903/05 Springfield rifle, .30-06 calibre, and M1907 leather sling.

BRITISH LIGHT MACHINE GUNNER, WESTERN FRONT, 1918

Steady increase in infantry firepower had brought to the rifle section its own automatic weapon. By 1916 all British battalions had 16 Lewis light machine guns. The Lewis gunners wore a lightened set of equipment, since they did not carry rifles. The overall appearance of the British Tommy in the desperate struggle of spring 1918 which stopped the German 'Michael' offensive, and in the final breakthrough of summer and autumn which forced Germany to negotiate, had however changed much less than that of his French and German counterparts, a testimony to the generally sound design of his kit and uniform.

1 - Mark 1 steel helmet. Second pattern with a crimped rim instead of a raw edge. The dull paint used for helmets varied in colour; the earlier helmets were generally finished in a drab greenish colour, the later ones in a yellower brown shade.

2 - M1902 service dress tunic. The last year of the war saw the widespread use of divisional signs sewn to the sleeves; in this case the red and green rose of the 55th (West Lancashire) Division. This first-line Territorial formation had been in France since January 1916, and distinguished itself in a stubborn stand at Givenchy-Festubert in April 1918. Brigade and battalion within the division were identified by geometric patches displayed on the back below the collar, and thus hidden here. On the left forearm, the embroidered skill-at-arms badge identifies a qualified Lewis gunner.

3 - Leather jerkin, worn from the winter of 1914/15 onwards, and almost universally issued in bad weather thereafter. It was made usually with four large panels but sometimes from off-cuts. Lined with khaki woollen material, or sometimes with fleece, it was durable, comfortable and popular. The classic pattern is illustrated, made of four panels of a russet brown shade, and fastened by four large leather-covered buttons.

4 - Light personal equipment, here based on the M1914 leather set described on p. 22. Instead of the rifle ammunition pouches, this light machine gunner has an open-topped holster and an ammunition pouch for his personal sidearm. The holster and 12-round pouch could also be attached to the M1908 webbing equipment belt and braces. The belt, braces, entrenching tool, haversack and canteen carrier are as on p.3. Again, note that the leather covering of the canteen is nonstandard.

5 - Webley Mark VI revolver, .455 in. calibre; while other makes were issued, this was the regulation sidearm from 1915 for officers and specialist troops who did not carry rifles. This large weapon is secured by a lanyard engaging with the butt ring.

6 - M1917 Small box respirator. The final pattern of WWI British gasmask, this much superior design remained in use until the middle of World War II. A mask of strong rubberised cloth with two glass eye pieces was connected by a corrugated rubber tube to the metal filter. The latter remained permanently in the canvas haversack, whose adjustable fabric strap allowed it to be carried on the chest in action. The haversack was slung round the body when out of action, or on top of the knapsack on the march.

7 - M1902 service dress trousers.

8 - Brown serge puttees.

9 - Ammunition boots. In 1918, a variant with a toe cap was also issued.

10 - Lewis light machine gun, .303 in. calibre. This air-cooled weapon was the standard light automatic weapon of the last three years of the war. The barrel was surrounded by a large cooling sleeve. It was fed by 47-round drum magazines, carried either in special webbing pouches replacing the cartridge carriers on the chest, or in canvas bucket-style bags by other members of the section. At more than 15 kg, the gun itself was enough of a load for the gunner. Its rate of fire, at 550 rounds per minute, was a welcome support for the rifle sections; unfortunately the Lewis gun was prone to jamming.

U.S. INFANTRYMAN, FRENCH 157th DIVISION, JULY 1918

T he question of including Black troops in the American Expeditionary Force caused the US Government some embarrassment in an age of racial segregation and unthinking prejudice. Eventually the 92nd Division was formed from regiments of black infantrymen; and later contingents arrived in France to form the 93rd Division, at least on paper. In fact, the first four regiments (369th, 370th, 371st and 372nd Infantry) were seconded to the French army, and used to fill up the French 157th Division of general Goybet. The enlisted men and many officers of this division were black; the French, long used to a multi-racial colonial army, were less sensitive in these matters, and appreciated this useful reinforcement. For practical reasons the division was entirely equipped from French stocks, though retaining American uniforms.

1 - French M1915 helmet painted dull blue-grey, with a narrow brown leather chin strap. The French infantry badge, a flaming bomb with the cypher 'RF' (for République Française), is seen on all known photographs of the 157th Division. A special American badge for the French helmet exists, however it is doubtful it was ever worn.

2 - M1917 olive drab tunic, slightly simplified from the M1912 design but still with four patch pockets. The collar discs bore 'US' (right) and on the left the number of the regiment under the infantry's crossed muskets.

3 - M1892/1914 French equipment braces in brown leather; each of the three branches of the 'Y' was fitted with a detachable metal hook which engaged with a ring on the back of the cartridge pouches.

4 - M1916 French cartridge pouches in brown leather. Their shape had not changed since 1888, but the method of attachment, modified in 1905, reached its final form in 1916.

5 - French M1892 sidebag in light brown cloth, containing the daily ration and personal effects.

6 - M1877 French two-litre water bottle in tin-plated metal covered with reclaimed uniform cloth. The tin-plated cup's handle is held by one of the water bottle cork strings.

7 - French ARS type gasmask, the last model issued during the Great War, which appeared from November 1917. The fluted metal canister was painted brown.

8 - M1903/14 brown leather belt, with plain two prong buckle.

9 - M1915 bayonet, suspended from the left side of the belt in (obscured here) a brown leather Y-shaped M1888/1914 frog.

10 - M1912 semi-breeches in olive drab wool, loose at the thigh and tapered from the knee down. These had five pockets: two oblique front, two rear hip, and a right fob pocket. Loops round the waist band allowed their use with a web belt when in shirtsleeves.

11- M1917 canvas leggings, distinguishable from the earlier model by the side lacing and increased number of hooks and eyelets. In the black units both types of leggings and puttees were often seen worn together.

12 - M1917 French service shoes, flesh side out, and hobnailed outsole.

13 - French M1907/15 Berthier rifle, 8 mm calibre, with M1907/14 brown leather sling.

5   6

9

FRENCH LIGHT MACHINE GUNNER, SUMMER 1918

The French, like the British, recognised the importance of allocating basic infantry units their own automatic weapon from 1915 onwards. For the Germans, normally on the defensive in strong static positions, the heavy machine gun was more consistently suitable, and it was not until 1918 that they issued a lighter and more portable version. The French solution to the problem was the 'fusil-mitrailleur M1915 CSRG', the acronym standing for the inventors and manufacturer, Chauchat-Sutter-Ribeyrolles-Gladiator. Universally known as the 'Chauchat,' it was a mediocre weapon prone to stoppages, but still better than nothing at a time when infantry troops committed to major offensives desperately needed a better means of delivering firepower than bolt-action rifles. The Chauchat team normally consisted of two men, a No 1 and an ammunition carrier, who were burdened by 36 kg of ammunition, in addition to the 9 kg of the gun and their personal equipment. By Spring 1918 the team had been increased to four, with this load more sensibly parcelled out between them. By that date each rifle company had 12 Chauchats.

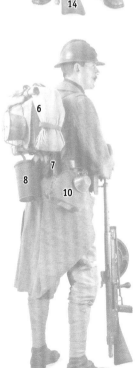

1 - M1915 helmet, painted blue-grey.

2 - Blue cotton stock.

3 - M1915 greatcoat in horizon blue. This pattern, which reverted to the traditional cut with two rows of six buttons, was issued to Metropolitan infantry regiments only during 1917 after stocks of the simplified M1914/15 had been exhausted. Here it bears the collar patches of the 122nd Infantry Regiment, in the new lozenge shape mandated in January 1917, surmounted by the red disc indicating the 2nd battalion. The four chevrons on the upper left sleeve are for two and a half years' service. Below this is a light machine gunner's skill-at-arms badge. This man has just been awarded the Croix de Guerre, a bronze star device indicating a mention in regimental despatches.

4 - M1892/14 equipment braces and M1903/14 belt in brown leather. The special equipment for Chauchat teams was compatible with these standard items.

5 - M1916/17 Chauchat magazine carriers, semi-circular in shape, each holding two magazines. Initially the curved side was worn inwards, but in May 1917 this was reversed, with a strap around the man's back to prevent them sliding down at the front under the weight of the magazines.

6 - M1917 special knapsack for LMG teams. Outwardly similar to the standard M1893, it had an internal metal frame to support the weight of 12 more magazines. Note the quick-release fastening on the right shoulder strap, allowing the gunner to drop his pack quickly and arrange his ammunition reserve close at hand when firing prone. The external stowage includes the tent section and blanket roll, the mess tin,

and a billhook. In theory the heavily burdened gunner was not supposed to carry an individual tool.

7 - M1916 pistol pouch. The Chauchat gunner's personal weapon was the 7.65 mm Ruby automatic pistol. This pouch, very similar to but slightly wider than the standard rifle ammunition pouch, had an internal spare magazine pocket.

8 - ARS gas mask canister, a fluted cylinder originally issued painted horizon blue, then brown as of 1918. The ARS ('Appareil respiratoire spécial') was issued from November 1917; it was a copy of the German gasmask, with a filter canister screwed to the face piece.

9 - M1892 sidebag in tan canvas.

10 - M1877 two-litre waterbottle and cup.

11 - M1914 semi-breeches, of standard cut but made of a thin ribbed smooth corduroy, sometimes issued for summer. Note the yellow infantry seam piping.

12 - Horizon blue wool puttees.

13 - M1917 ankle boots. The height was increased by about 15 mm that year, to give better support, but this modification made no real visible difference.

14 - M1915 Chauchat LMG. The 'Chauchat' was manufactured in haste by untried industrial processes (the maker, Gladiator, was in fact a bicycle manufacturer!). Nearly a quarter of a million were made, allowing for issue to the French from 1916, and to the AEF. But the 8 mm Lebel rimmed cartridge was unsuitable for the smooth feeding of automatic weapons. Its shape had also dictated the semi-circular design of the magazine.

GERMAN INFANTRYMAN, OCTOBER 1918

I n the spring of 1918, Germany launched a final offensive in the West, and by the use of surprise and of new, flexible tactics, succeeded in making serious gains before Amiens and on the Marne. However, by July this offensive had been brought to a halt thanks to superhuman efforts by the French and British armies, and particularly the fresh American divisions, which went on to the attack for the first time in May. Bled white in these summer battles, German units were composed more of adolescents of the classes of 1919 and 1920 than of seasoned veterans. In his appearance, too, the soldier of late 1918 bore little resemblance to the infantryman of 1914; only his field cap and bayonet knot enlivened a uniform which had evolved under battle conditions, where inconspicuous drabness was synonymous with survival. Our reconstruction, in full marching order for the long walk home, carries several items of wartime and substitute manufacture.

1 - M1910 field cap in field grey cloth, its band and piping in the distinctive infantry arm-of-service colour. Two pressed metal cockades are sewn to the front: that on the crown in the Imperial colours of black, white and red, and that on the band in the colours of the state, here the black and white of Prussia. This cap was only worn behind the lines after the first year or so of the war; in 1917 a universal pattern with a green band was introduced, but the old type continued in use, a drab cloth strip often hiding the red band.

2 - M1915 greatcoat in field grey, the large fall collar faced with green, as on the Bluse. This single-breasted garment closed down the front with six large uniform buttons, and had two large flapped pockets in the sides, set at a slant. Although often sewn down, the shoulder straps were officially of detachable type, and bore the same white infantry piping and red unit number or monogram as on the Bluse.

3 - M1916 steel helmet; here in monochrome grey, it was often painted with camouflage colours by 1918. Here it is hung from the belt by its M1891 chin strap.

4 - M1895 blackened leather belt. The M1915 grey painted plate is embossed with the Prussian design of crown and 'Gott Mit Uns' motto.

5 - Flashlight in black-painted metal, a non-regulation item sometimes attached to a coat button by a leather tab, or, as here, slipped onto the belt.

6 - M1909 cartridge pouches of ersatz manufacture in vulcanised fibre. They held four charger clips in each of the three pockets, for a total load of 120 rounds.

7 - M1895 knapsack, here of simplified wartime manufacture in greyish canvas. It accommodated reserve rations and changes of clothing. The M1892 tent section is rolled round the pack and held with leather straps. A wartime-made M1910 mess tin is strapped to the pack flap.

8 - M1887 breadbag in the greyish fabric often seen on equipment of wartime manufacture.

9 - M1907 enamelled water bottle, covered with reclaimed brown corduroy. The attachment system has been simplified to a single tab and hook attached to one of the breadbag rings.

10 - M1893 cup. Green-enamelled metal was now used in place of aluminium. It is attached by a handle to one of the breadbag's belt suspension loops. It was theoretically stowed inside the bag, however.

11 - M1917 gasmask, in its grey-painted carrier slung by a fabric strap.

12 - M1887 portable entrenching spade. The scabbard of the M1915 bayonet is secured to it by a strap. Note the 'Troddel,' or bayonet knot, in company colours.

13 - Surprisingly at this date, this young soldier is shod with a pair of **M1866 knee boots**, the tan leather being blackened according to regulations.

14 - M1898 Mauser rifle, 7.92 mm calibre, with a wartime sling made of grey fabric with leather tips.

7

10

11

8

9

12

UNITED STATES MARINE, WESTERN FRONT, 1918

In 1918, the US Marines already enjoyed a reputation as an élite corps specialising in overseas operations, and proud of their differences with the Army. It was only natural that the Marines should provide an early contingent for the AEF, and the 'Leathernecks' made up the 4th (Marine) Brigade of the 2nd Division (5th and 6th Marines, 6th Marine Machine Gun Battalion). If at first glance their uniform and equipment appeared identical to the Army's, there were in fact many small differences born of a fierce and exclusive esprit de corps. These differences became less noticeable as convenience mandated the resupply of the Marine brigade from Army stocks. Our subject is shown in the original 'forest green' uniform worn by reinforcements arriving directly from the USA. Upholding their traditions, the Marines played a major part in stopping the German offensive of May-June 1918 before Paris, and suffered heavy casualties.

1 - M1918 Overseas cap in olive drab wool; there was no 'forest green' version of this headgear. On the left front is pinned the Corps emblem of eagle, globe and anchor, normally worn on the M1914 hat.

2 - M1914 tunic in forest green wool. The standing collar bore no insignia. The garment closed down the front with five large eagle and anchor buttons, and had four patch pockets with pointed and buttoned flaps, the skirt pockets being bellowed. Note the pointed cuffs and the marksman's badge above the left breast pocket, a distinction achieved by some 70% of combat Marines in 1918.

3 - 'Liberty light', an electric lamp carried in a cloth pouch attached by a tab to a tunic's buttonhole.

4 - Ammunition bandolier, the five pockets each holding two five-round clips for the .30-06 Springfield rifle.

5 - Cartridge belt, very similar to the Army's M1910; differences included the USMC emblem on the press studs, and the stronger green shade of the webbing. Each of the ten pouches held two five-round clips.

6 - M1910 first aid packet pouch, used by both Army and Marines; the packet was however the Navy pattern.

7 - Navy and Marine Corps model Mills webbing suspenders, hooked to the eyelets of the belt.

8 - M1910 water bottle and carrier, differing from Army issue again by the press studs bearing the Corps emblem, and being marked 'USMC' on the inside.

9 - M1917 trench knife.

10 - M1905 bayonet in its M1910 fabric and leather scabbard. This was standard issue to all AEF infantry units.

11 - M1917 gasmask, copied from the British pattern. Here it is carried slung in the back.

12 - M1917 helmet in manganese steel; the lining was made of oilcloth, the chin strap in brown leather. The example illustrated is painted forest green.

13 M1914 trousers in forest green wool. Cut straight, rather than as semi-breeches, these trousers had two slash side pockets and belt loops.

14 - Puttees of olive drab cloth, identical to the Army issue, though it is possible that forest green puttees have existed.

15 - M1917 service shoes, common to the entire AEF.

16 - M1903/05 Springfield rifle, .30-06 calibre, with 'No-buckl' patent web sling. The action is protected by a canvas cover closed by press studs.

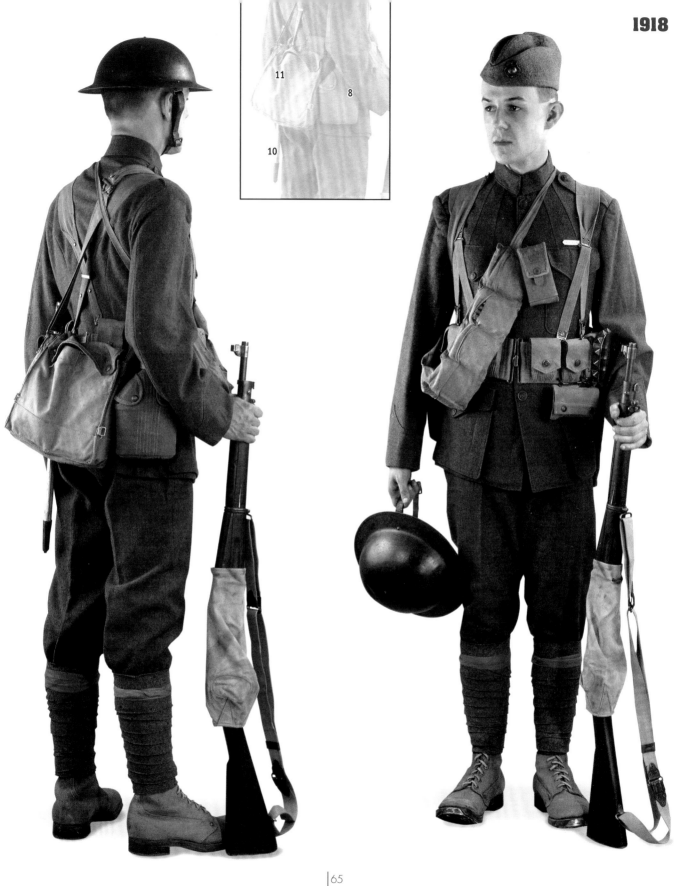

11

8

10

Contents

Acknowledgements

The gathering of such a large number of original World War One uniforms and items of equipment would have been impossible without the generous collaboration of many private collectors and museums throughout Europe.

We wish to express our gratitude to:

— *British Army:* Laurent Mirouze and David Bardiaux, curator of the Musée de la Targette, Neuville-St-Vaast
— *German Army:* Georges Bailly and Robert Bullock
— *French Army:* Laurent Mirouze, François Vauvillier and Jean Pierre Verney
— *US Army:* Georges Bailly
— *Italian & Austrian Armies:* Furio Lazzarini and Franco Mesturini
— *Belgian Army:* M. Jacobs, curator of the Musée Royal de l'Armée, Brussels (1990)
— *Russian Army:* Gérard Gorokhoff.

Photo Credits

Toni Bergamo (pp. 21, 33, 41, 43, 45); Stefan Ciejka (pp. 7, 13, 19, 27, 35, 49, 53, 59, 63); Laurent Mirouze (pp. 5, 37, 39, 51, 55, 65); François Vauvillier (pp. 9, 11, 15, 17, 23, 25, 29, 31, 47, 57, 61).

Series editor: Philippe Charbonnier.
Design and layout by Philippe Charbonnier and Jean-Marie Mongin.

ISBN: 978-2-35250-268-5
Publisher's number: 35250
© Histoire & Collections 2013

Histoire & Collections
SA au capital de 182 938,82 €
5, avenue de la République
F-75541 Paris Cédex 11-France
Tel: +33(1) 40 21 18 20 / Fax: +33(1) 47 00 51 11
www.histoireetcollections.com

This book has been designed, typed, laid-out and processed by *Histoire & Collections* on fully integrated computer equipment. Color separation: *Studio A&C*

Printed by Calidad Grafica, Spain, European Union.
January 2013.